THE
ENGLISH HOUSE

English Country Houses & Interiors

First published in the United States of America in 2004 by

Rizzoli International Publications, Inc.

300 Park Avenue South

New York, NY 10010

www.rizzoliusa.com

Originally published in the UK by Scriptum Editions

565 Fulham Road, London, SW6 1ES

Created by Co & Bear Productions (UK) Ltd.

Copyright · 2004 Co & Bear Productions (UK) Ltd.

Photographs copyright · 2004 Simon McBride

Co & Bear Productions (UK) Ltd identify Judith Wilson as author of the work.

Publishers Beatrice Vincenzini, Francesco Venturi

Executive Director David Shannon

Art Director Pritty Ramjee

Publishing Assistant Ruth Deary

Printed and bound by Officine Grafiche DeAgostini, Italy

Color Reproduction Bright Arts Graphics, Singapore

First edition

10 9 8 7 6 5 4 3 2 1

ISBN 0-8478-2647-3

Library of Congress Catalog Control Number 2004104621

THE
ENGLISH HOUSE

English Country Houses & Interiors

SALLY GRIFFITHS AND
SIMON MCBRIDE

CONTENTS

INTRODUCTION

What is an English house? More powerful than the conventional chocolate-box image of a thatched cottage with roses round its door, our vision of what epitomizes the English house might be a country mansion encircled by parkland or a stone-built Georgian rectory backed by churchyard yews, a beamed Tudor manor house or stucco-fronted Regency villa. It might even be a fanciful folly built on a rich landowner's whim.

The English house is as much a part of its landscape as mature woodlands and rolling pasture, the surprise of a church spire, or a cluster of farm buildings. There are houses constructed from every material, from local hewn stone to ancient timbers or rendered façades, roofed with traditional slate or thatch or tiles. In this catholic mix of styles, from classical Palladian architecture to Gothic detailing, Georgian symmetry to the age-old charm of a cruck-built cottage, it is impossible to single out just one style that sums up our national architectural heritage.

The evolution of the English house may at first seem clear-cut. Up until the seventeenth century, timber-framed houses were the norm, until stone-built dwellings became increasingly popular. Details such as Tudor stone mullions or Georgian sash windows may initially define a house as belonging to a particular period, but, over centuries, buildings are adapted - a room added here, a fresh façade put on there - to keep pace with architectural fashions and changing social patterns. Preserving buildings in their original form is a twentieth-century innovation.

Once we see that period houses are a patchwork of eras and architectural styles, it becomes a voyage of discovery to pinpoint the earliest original features, and the most recent additions. Questions arise. Why was a new wing added at a particular time? Who decided to raze a close-by cottage to the ground? Why was a fifteenth-century hall built on the foundations of an even earlier house - was this especially fertile land, or simply well screened from prevailing winds? Despite England's long history of detailed record-keeping - many of its old houses are plotted on old ordnance survey maps or even noted in the Domesday Book - not every question will be answered. And does that matter? Every house, perhaps, should be allowed to retain a sense of mystery.

It is telling that, in picturing our ideal of the English house, we hark back to the past, not yet to the present or future. England has a rich heritage of twentieth-century architecture, from Sir Edwin Lutyens's great country properties to the clean-lined 1930s designs of architects Connell, Ward and Lucas, and the more radical modern buildings of architects like Sir Richard Rogers and John Pawson. But the English in the main remain loyal to buildings

RIGHT *In Ann Mollo's London townhouse, a first-floor room is dedicated to a purpose-built library. The Victorian Gothic cupboards have been specially designed to feature pull-out book rests.*

rooted in the past. If, in part, that's because we rejoice in what we know, it's also because a house with a history has true character. Any new owner of a period property, or a family who has, for generations, lived in the same home, will revel in regional myths, old photographs and drawings, and the memories of local village people. The English house is the sum of many parts, in which history plays a vital role.

To find out more about an English house, we must open the doors and look within, into its heart. Walk through the front door, and the delights are sensual. There will be the mellow scent of beeswax polish, perhaps freshly cut garden flowers, or the damp smell of dogs, just returned from a walk. Go upstairs, and there's the smoothness of a wooden handrail, polished by the touch of ten thousand hands, and the time-worn central indentation in the treads. A panelled door may not fit snugly to keep out all draughts, but there's pleasure in holding its brass knob, which has been grasped for two centuries and more. There's satisfaction, too, in the slope of wide, old floorboards in an attic bedroom, or a charmingly uneven door frame that has stood the test of time. In today's modern world, where the fabric of new buildings is mass-produced and uniform to the eye, the irregularity of line is particularly appealing.

RIGHT *The double doors at the north entrance to Elizabeth Gage's converted school house are flanked by a pair of Gothic urns, and modern iron nautilus shell style chairs, brought by her from America.*

And just as the structure of an English house is rarely homogeneous, neither are its contents. The paintings and chests, mirrors, candlesticks, textiles and chairs must be a mix of periods and styles, accumulated over generations. This is the English way. We don't easily embrace the new. Typically, old country houses are an eclectic mix of the occasional purchase and the inherited piece, the inevitable white elephants, the much-loved, the valuable and the rustic. Over generations, furniture is mended, re-upholstered, altered or cut down, as it moves from one home to the next. In the English house, there is a tradition of make-do and mend, and a genteel art to tossing a wool throw over a threadbare silk sofa, pleasure in preserving pretty things as they once were many years ago.

The English are great collectors - of the precious, the exotic or the just plain eccentric. The visitor will expect to find floor-to-ceiling bookshelves stuffed with books, mantelpieces crowded with antique china, from eighteenth-century creamware to a rare piece of Spode, antique sideboards stacked with old silver salt cellars and cream jugs, rummers and decanters, and boot rooms equipped with old wicker baskets and a motley array of walking sticks. Collections personally amassed, and lovingly displayed, are as much part of the interior character as flowers planted in the garden, or chintz hanging at the windows.

English houses are good places to come home to. Of course we have moved on from the days of the Tudor hall, where everything, from communal meals to the welcoming of guests, took place. Over the centuries, the hall has diminished in size, and from the early eighteenth century, the focus shifted to a series of smaller entertaining rooms; these are still the template today for the formal drawing room and dining room. Yet in a sense, we have come full circle. Now, the concept for the great hall has been reinvented as the big family kitchen, with its ubiquitous cooking range, scrubbed pine table and comfortable sofa. In the contemporary English house, it is the kitchen that visitors make for and that forms the focus of family life.

Yet if, in the early twentieth-first century, the way we inhabit and use the English house has changed, those alterations are - in the scale of things - barely perceptible. A bathroom may be installed where a dressing room once was, a room opened up or a doorway moved, but over decades, centuries, such alterations are slow and gentle, so that a house evolves organically over time. In the country, away from fast-changing urban fashions, this is particularly predictable. Looking back, we must be grateful for that slow change, as it allows us to keep one foot in the present and the other, firmly in the past.

It is from this sense of history at a domestic level that organizations such as English Heritage, the National Trust and the Society for the Protection of Ancient Buildings arose, and bodies like the Georgian Society and the Victorian Society were formed. Many of the houses in this book are designated by English Heritage as listed buildings (graded I, the highest, II* or II), protecting their historic fabric but also restricting change and modernization.

Perhaps because major structural changes are often tightly controlled, not to mention our passionate desire to preserve the past, it is often the gardens of the English house that undergo most rigorous change. For some owners, that will mean restoring the strict symmetry of Elizabethan parterres, in tune with the architectural period of the building. For others, it is about a series of outdoor sanctuaries, from a leafy grotto to a manicured croquet lawn, or creating a scented profusion of English roses and perennial borders. How exciting it is to discover, among an overgrown wilderness, ancient statues or fountains, or a 'lost' pool, ripe for restoration.

Whether highly stylized or picturesquely overblown, a tiny patch of land or stretching to the horizon, the garden becomes an integral part of every house's architecture. Even city-dwellers lovingly tend a backyard filled with honeysuckle and roses. We are a nation of gardeners, to whom it is second nature to anchor each house to the greater outdoors. Given the vagaries of the weather, that link may be practical, or purely visual - what counts is a view of greenery, and the promise of an escape outdoors.

The English house is a place with a welcome, a home stamped with the character of its current inhabitants, as well as the imprint of owners stretching way back into the past. It is a place where families are raised, friendships conducted, a place where the simplicities and intricacies of daily life goes on. The English house has a purpose for being there, with a present, a history and - most importantly - a future waiting to unfold.

TUDOR MANOR HOUSE

Some of the grand – and the not quite so grand – English period houses are easily spotted from a country road. Perhaps a property was built on a hillside, to be admired, or to get the best possible view across the landscape. Others may be spied a distance off, discreetly screened by woodlands and surrounding parkland. Then there are some houses so deeply embedded in the countryside that you would never get to see them, unless you deliberately sought them out. Owlpen Manor, in Gloucestershire, is such a house. Set into the lea of a valley, backed by a beech wood, it looks out benignly on to meadowland, with the village Church of the Holy Cross standing just behind. Visitors don't chance upon Owlpen. They must travel a steep one-mile wooded drive just to catch a glimpse of its imposing gabled façade.

Owlpen's owner, Nicholas Mander, comments that this sheltered spot is 'a good site for living', and according to the house's very own guidebook, there's been a dwelling on the spot for at least 800 years, long before the current house was built. Even today, the springs on the site still naturally emerge into the gardens. Owlpen is a Tudor manor, built from local Cotswold limestone, conceived and built in the fifteenth century by the Olepenne family and added to over the centuries between 1420 and the early eighteenth century. It's a comparatively small manor house, yet what it lacks in size, it makes up for in historical significance. All but abandoned as a dwelling in about 1803, it was eventually 'repaired' and inhabited again in the 1920s. Small wonder, then, that much of its original architecture has remained intact.

Nicholas and Karin Mander bought Owlpen in 1974. Now that their five children have grown up, they open the house to the public in the summer. Rather charmingly, the guidebook urges the interested visitor to 'indulge a little untidiness and household clutter', a phrase remarkably absent from guides to some grander stately homes. It was Nicholas who first wanted to purchase Owlpen, because he had a passion for early houses.

'But I sensed that there were the makings of a way of life here,' he comments. Slowly, he and Karin have bought back much of the old estate land and now run it as a business, with a farm, woodland, restaurant and nine holiday cottages in the grounds.

Like so many English houses, Owlpen has evolved over the centuries. Stand in the formal Stuart garden, looking up at the grand south façade, and its three gables look remarkably homogenous. But look a little closer (Owlpen guidebook in hand) and it's possible to see that each block is almost a century apart. Despite its Georgian sash windows, the easternmost gable dates back to the fifteenth century. The rendered central block was built in 1540, while the west wing bears the datestone 'Anno 1616 TD'. Astoundingly, aside from the eighteenth-century 'improvements', this is the newest part of the house.

Yet it's not until you walk around to the east-facing entrance that Owlpen's fifteenth-century origins are truly apparent. Built in 1450, the elevation looks more like a farmhouse, with mediaeval timbered windows and a low, wooden entrance door. Enter the Cotswold flagstoned hall, and to the right there's the early seventeenth-century kitchen block, probably built where more ancient service outbuildings once stood. The modern kitchen is now housed here. Turn to the left, and you are in what is called the 'east service wing'. These days, the old pantry serves as a ticket office for summer visitors. Centuries ago, it was at the catering heart of the Tudor manor house.

What is most fascinating about Owlpen is that, once you pass into the main living spaces - the Great Hall in the central block, the Oak Parlour in the west wing and the Little Parlour in the east wing - the layout is remarkably modern. The central, rectangular Great Hall, which would once have been the place to eat and be convivial, still holds the dining table and a piano, and is used by the family for Sunday lunches and on high days and holidays. And, like modern open-plan living, the Little Parlour (now called the drawing room) and the Oak Parlour (the family's cosy TV room) both lead sociably off. Nicholas, a fount of knowledge on Tudor living patterns, explains that this arrangement is 'based on the mediaeval principle of one room leading into the next'.

Yet, however contemporary the layout, it's not easy, one suspects, to turn what is essentially a living museum into a family home. Owlpen, of course, is Grade I listed, so any alteration has had to be done with sensitivity. The five bathrooms, for example, were squeezed into what were dressing rooms, 'once used for putting on wigs and the all-too-occasional hip bath'. In the two main reception rooms, it has been a case of combining a mix of comfortable, yet early, antiques appropriate to the period, chiefly passed down as family heirlooms, and enjoying the ancient surroundings. Nicholas isn't surprised that it's so easy to live here. 'The house has responded to human needs for such a long time that it doesn't impose,' he comments. 'Architecturally, it's an organic house.'

Although the changes may have been radical at the time, the mix of early eighteenth-century painted panelling and sash windows in the Little Parlour and the quartered oak panelling and lattice windows in the Oak Parlour seems a particularly happy one. There is a visual contrast, of course, most evident from the Great Hall, where the wooden door leading into the low-ceilinged Oak Parlour faces the elaborate Italianate-style, arched door frame (constructed in 1722) of the drawing room entrance. But as, over the decades, the Manders have filled their living space with pretty antique furniture and family portraits, all the rooms blend to a seamless whole.

Luckily for the Manders, two twists of fate in Owlpen's history prevented too many major changes. The Daunt family (1462–1815) were responsible for the building as we see it today, but when Mary Daunt married Thomas Stoughton in 1815, they built a new mansion on the hill for their family home. Owlpen was effectively mothballed for the next hundred years, although the gardens were kept up, for picnics and summer outings. Eventually, Norman Jewson, having heard of the 'beautiful and romantically situated old house' from friends in the area, bought Owlpen in 1925. Also a passionate lover of ancient houses (and an

LEFT *A short flight of semi-circular stone steps leads down from the formal parterres in front of the south façade. The panelled stone gate piers, dated 1720, were, as late as the 1940s, flanked by the original wooden palisade.*

active member of the Society for the Protection of Ancient Buildings) he set about sensitively repairing the property, rather than trying to modernize it.

It's a moot point whether all his changes were successful. The elm floor he laid in the Little Parlour was so thick that the dado rail appears too low, compromising the classical proportions of the wall panelling. On the other hand, there have been charming additions. An Arts and Crafts fan, Jewson added many plaster mouldings, one of which - an owl - sits above the door into the Oak Parlour. He also took many photographs and did sketches of the building, which remain a valuable record.

It is upstairs, perhaps, where there is more marked separation between the family's living quarters and the 'public' rooms. Visitors don't make it to the Manders' bedroom 'because it's full of clutter!' but are directed to the two most historic bed chambers. The Solar Chamber (1616) sits above the Oak Parlour, and from its crooked mullioned bay window you can look out on to the formal parterre gardens, painstakingly recreated by the Manders. Above the Great Hall is Queen Margaret's Room, so named because Queen Margaret of Anjou, wife of Henry VI, is said to have slept there during the Wars of the Roses. In here hang 'lively painted cloths', some of the few items still remaining at Owlpen when the Manders moved in. These distempered canvas panels are a unique survival, probably late seventeenth century, and depict scenes from the biblical story of Joseph and his brothers.

On window sills and in a glass-fronted cabinet in the solar are displays of everything from glass-beaded purses to old clay pipes. The medley is, says Nicholas Mander, symptomatic of the Mander passion for collecting. An ordinary-looking assortment of beer and cider bottles holds particular significance. Unearthed from the midden behind one of the barns, they are a reminder, not just of local breweries, but of earlier, simpler, lives.

LEFT & ABOVE *Passing between a pair of ancient stone piers with 'biretta' finials brings you to the east front of the house, where Owlpen's mediaeval origins are evident from the uneven window arrangement and the low timber door. The canted bay windows of the west wing are a particularly distinguished feature, as the attic window diminishes to fit the gable.*

LEFT & ABOVE, OPPOSITE

The timber door in the east wing has been dated to 1450, while the wrought iron hinges and latch are thought to be early eighteenth century. The door bell is a 1920s Norman Jewson addition. Affectionately known as the garden door, the south entrance is surprisingly modest. The door is dated 1540.

OVERLEAF

The roof to the east wing is tiled in the traditional Cotswold manner, with 'diminishing courses'. The original fifteenth-century roof has been heavily patched and repaired over the centuries.

ABOVE & RIGHT

A view of the entrance hall in the east wing. To one side of the front door sits an early Georgian settle bench, and beyond that is a 1680 coffer, which once belonged to William Morris. The floor is of traditional polished Cotswold flagstones. The seventeenth-century newel stairs wind up to the first floor from one corner of the Oak Parlour. Directly above, in the west wing, is the solar chamber.

ABOVE

A view from the Great Hall, looking through into the drawing room (once called the Little Parlour). Above the piano hangs a portrait of one of Nicholas Mander's ancestors, Jemima Mander, dated 1780. The elaborate Italianate doorway was built in 1722 by Henry Fryer, probably of Bristol. It was reduced in height in 1926, when Norman Jewson laid a new flagstone floor, thus altering the original proportions.

RIGHT

The drawing room retains its early eighteenth-century panelling, installed by Thomas Daunt V, complete with a buffet recess bearing traces of original paint and gilding. Today, there is an assortment of early antique furniture, including a Queen Anne wing chair. Above the fireplace hangs an eighteenth-century pastel portrait by John Russell.

ABOVE

The Manders have a family history of collecting. Here, there is a selection of eighteenth- and nineteenth-century decorative glass-beaded purses, acquired by Nicholas Mander's great-grandmother. The desk in the Oak Parlour is clustered with many family photographs, old and recent.

OPPOSITE

In the Oak Parlour, housed in the west wing, the family now have a snug sitting room, with sofas upholstered in faded damask, or covered with antique tapestry cushions and throws. The original 1616 quartered oak panelling is still in place, and bears traces of early attempts at graining. In one corner hangs a floor-to-ceiling portrait of Nicholas Mander's great-grandfather, Alderman Sir Charles Tertius Mander, painted in 1896.

OPPOSITE

In the mid sixteenth-century first-floor bedroom, dubbed Queen Margaret's Room, there are some fine examples of early painted cloths. Such cloths were common in Tudor and Stuart interiors, and were hand-painted in distemper on to unbleached canvas linen strips. In front of the cloth, by the window, stands a French Marot-style tapestry chair, and to its right, there's a working spinning wheel.

ABOVE & RIGHT

The entrance to Queen Margaret's Room is via a double door frame, and the panelled door still bears its original sixteenth-century iron door furniture. In the same bedroom, there's a mid-Georgian painted bed in Cuban mahogany. The painted cloth behind depicts a biblical scene, showing Joseph being sold by his brothers to merchants for twenty pieces of silver.

BELOW & RIGHT

The Solar Chamber, originally built in 1616 as the principal bedroom on the first floor of the west wing, is used today as a spare bedroom. It has been furnished with a German marriage bed, and to the left of the bed stands Nicholas Mander's great-grandmother's mahogany wardrobe, dated 1870. From the bay mullion window, there are views across the formal parterre garden. On the deep stone window sill sits a fossil of a scallop shell, found in the hills behind the house, and a fragment of encaustic tile, as used on the floor of Owlpen church.

ABOVE & RIGHT

Owlpen's gardens, entered by decorative wrought iron gates, are defined by formal gravel paths. A view from the house, looks directly down on to the formal parterre. The gardens were laid out by the Manders in 1983, in sympathy with the original Stuart garden (its paths still lie beneath the modern gravel). The beds around the lawns, with their clipped box borders, are planted with cottage garden plants, aromatics and old shrub roses.

VICTORIAN SCHOOL HOUSE

Overlooking the village green, tucked between a quiet country lane and an enclosed shady garden, Graham Carr's Dorset home seems to be the quintessential country retreat. To curious passers-by, peeping over the wall, it's a modest single-storey Victorian building of brick and stone, characterized by two tall windows framed within tiled Gothic arches, an ordinary brick chimney and a sharply pitched roof. Only the older generation in the village would know that this was once the village school house, finally closed in 1981 due to a sharply dwindling population in an agricultural community. Only locals, too, would know that the house was originally funded by money supplied by the village church, which still stands at the corner of the lane.

Today, it's the home of Graham Carr, who charmingly describes himself as an interior decorator, artist, and furniture and garden designer, all rolled into one. If the English have always had a flair for the eccentric, be that in the arts, fashion or design, then his home must surely be the perfect example. Step into the hall, and then on through a 'secret' jib door into the vaulted central room, and you are transported into a colourful, highly decorative interior. 'The very exoticism of the house is peculiarly English,' Graham comments. 'It's a look we do very well.' He lives alone, with his Irish water spaniel, Ozzie (named after the equally outlandish Osbert Sitwell), and confesses that, after twenty years here, he wouldn't - couldn't - live anywhere else.

Press him as to the origins of his home, and very little, he confesses, is known. The architect remains a mystery, but according to the deeds, the school house is built on land donated by three or four local landowners, for the good of the village children. The building was completed in 1849, and is still attached to what was originally the school master's house. In those days, the two were linked via a door in the north wall of the main room, but this has long since been blocked up. The building is Gothic-inspired, probably because it was church-funded, but was designed along simple and strong

Victorian lines, rather than in the earlier, more fantastical Gothick eighteenth-century interpretation.

Given Graham's predilection for the dramatic, the school house provided him with an ideal shell for a new home. When he viewed it, back in 1983, it was both convenient, because it was close to his workshop, and had plenty of potential. The main room (the original school room) measures 6 by 9 m (20 by 30 ft), with a ceiling reaching up to nearly 8 m (25 ft), so the generous proportions appealed. It has two vast windows, facing east and south, presumably installed to coax in maximum light for Victorian pupils. Even better, it was effectively derelict, having been used as an ad hoc library after the school closed. 'I just knew I had to have it!' exclaims Graham. Although it dates from the the mid nineteenth century, it isn't a listed building, so there were fewer constraints as to what he could, or could not, add or take away.

Today, it is tempting to search for tell-tale signs of the old school within the main room, but regrettably none remain. The tiny cloakroom at the north corner of the building, with its rows of basins, has been converted into Graham's kitchen. The outside school toilets, still there when he moved in, are also long gone. And in the centre of the west wall, where Graham presumes the old oil stove would once have stood, is a new open hearth, with wooden fire surround and over-mantel mirror, made to his own design. The only lasting clue to the room's original purpose lies in the unusually high setting of one of the

big windows - designed, he suspects, to prevent idle children gazing outside. When Graham replaced the windows (the wooden frames were rotten) he had them faithfully copied to the original design, but elongated the south-facing one and dropped it lower into the brickwork.

Outside, there are equally few traces of the school's origins. The small garden, barely more than 9 m (30 ft) square, still looked much like a derelict playground when Graham moved in. These days there are paths and patios prettily paved by him in herringbone brick and decorative, circular cobblestone designs, and the gardens are chiefly topiary and low box hedges. 'Consequently they look better in the winter than in the summer!' remarks Graham. Scan the exterior of the building, and there's just one reminder of its earlier life. High up on the south gable, housed beneath a white timber canopy, hangs the old school bell. It might still ring, Graham muses, were it not for the blackbirds who regularly nest there.

The English have always been adept at making the most of their homes, however humble, and Graham has extracted maximum potential from his. Faced with fashioning a cosy interior from one vast vaulted

OPPOSITE *The large, south-facing window of the 1849 school house lets sunshine flood into the main room. Above the restored window frames and surrounds, Graham added diamond-shaped tiles similar in shape to the original scallop ones, many of which were missing.*

room, he chose to build a mezzanine floor at one end, accessed by a spiral staircase. The more intimate space beneath it is an ideal spot for the dining table and chairs. Lesser decorators in search of authenticity might have used a plain timber balcony to fence off the sleeping platform, to match the soaring ceiling beams, but not Graham. Instead, he brought back carved wood panels from India, and installed a canopied walnut Portuguese bed. From the dining area beneath the mezzanine, you can turn to the right, through a rusticated brick doorway that leads outside, or left, to the kitchen, where the children's cloakroom once stood.

Yet perhaps it's not so much the extraordinary space that dominates, but the unexpected collision of vibrant colours, textures and patterns. Ever the artist, Graham is not one for subdued English eau de nil and creams, and is instead a lover of the exotic and bold. Walls once hung with little more than a blackboard and world map are these days decorated with a two-tone hand-painted stripe in vermilion and cherry, overpainted by Graham with an exuberant tree of life design. (This is the second version: when he first moved in, his theme was stencilled, overblown damask.) The original floorboards, which the builder

had advised Graham to rip up, were carefully treated and then painted with a marbled trellis pattern, with an antique Persian rug thrown on top. Above the windows hung with striped ottoman curtains the Gothic-inspired scalloped and painted pelmets are sprinkled with gold.

In a more recent ground-floor extension, which Graham built to house an extra bedroom, bathroom and study, the colours are equally enticing. You enter via a tiny hall, which has butter yellow painted walls. From here, you pass left into his bedroom, its walls lined in blue and white Kashmiri crewelwork (also brought back from India), its bed hung with more of the same. Then you can gaze straight into a small bathroom, with its burnt orange walls and colourful Burmese religious scrolls, or left into his tiny office, which is a subtler shade of pale blue. 'I find colour interesting,' says Graham. 'I couldn't live without it.'

What also makes this house so appealing is that it is an intriguing melting pot of furniture and decorative objects culled from many assorted periods and styles. Just as the eighteenth-century Englishman

ABOVE & OPPOSITE *The bow-fronted stone trough comes from the north of England, and is decorated with a French iron bird. The herringbone bricks of the terrace were chosen to retain the feel of the Victorian brick and stone architecture. The garden furniture includes an unusual pair of nineteenth-century wire English chairs and a twentieth-century metal bench. The table, designed by Graham, is made from a stone slab sitting on a saddle stone.*

once returned from his Grand Tour with European treasures, or families repatriated from India after the days of the Raj brought back colonial mementoes, Graham has gathered a fabulous assortment of beautiful things. No matter, he laughingly admits, that his Chinese figures come from Gloucestershire, and his African masks from the flea markets in Paris, where he regularly goes on antiques-buying trips. No matter, either, that the seventeenth-century painting of a girl, probably Mexican, was found in Madrid, or that the modern painting in the hall hails from Ibiza. What counts is the interior's rich character, and as a sensory experience, it's hard to beat.

So in the main room, the big sofa is new, but the tapestry chairs flanking it are 1730s, still clad in their original blue and white needlepoint. The low table is antique Indian, but has been painted by Graham in an exotic Islamic design of stylized flowers. The gold panels hanging either side of the south window are Chinese, bearing raised good luck symbols, but the chandeliers are late eighteenth-century French crystal. Over time, Graham has bought over-sized and dramatic pieces specifically for the main room, but says it's an organic process, too. 'I'm an antiques dealer, so things catch my eye, and pieces come and go,' he comments. But one thing is sure: there will be no more structural additions, inside or out. The old school house may not be listed, but Graham has remained faithful to its origins. 'It's safe in my hands for some time to come,' he concludes.

LEFT & ABOVE

The grand drawing room, with its lofty ceiling, was once the village school room. It is now home to a combination of furniture and accessories that perfectly reflect Graham's fascination with the colourful and the exotic. A pair of 1730s French chairs, still with their original needlepoint upholstery, stands at either end of an antique Indian coffee table, repainted by Graham with an Islamic-inspired-design. The sofa is clustered with a rich mix of cushions, covered in Japanese silk, Morrocan needlework and African tribal prints. On the walls, flanking the far window, hang a pair of gilded Chinese panels bearing good luck symbols, while the metal support of an eighteenth-century French chandelier hanging from the vaulted ceiling is twisted metal for extra reflection.

ABOVE

The tall-backed dining chairs were made to Graham's design, and the table is covered with a hand-blocked Indian floor cloth. The dining table is tucked beneath the bedroom mezzanine, which is accessed by the spiral staircase in the corner.

RIGHT

On either side of the fireplace sits a pair of nineteenth-century oak console tables. These hold ever-changing displays of artefacts culled from around the world. In front of a seventeenth-century portrait of a girl, there are Han dynasty ceramic geese teamed with figurines by the contemporary ceramicist, Alison Stewart. The carving on the far right is a tribal African piece.

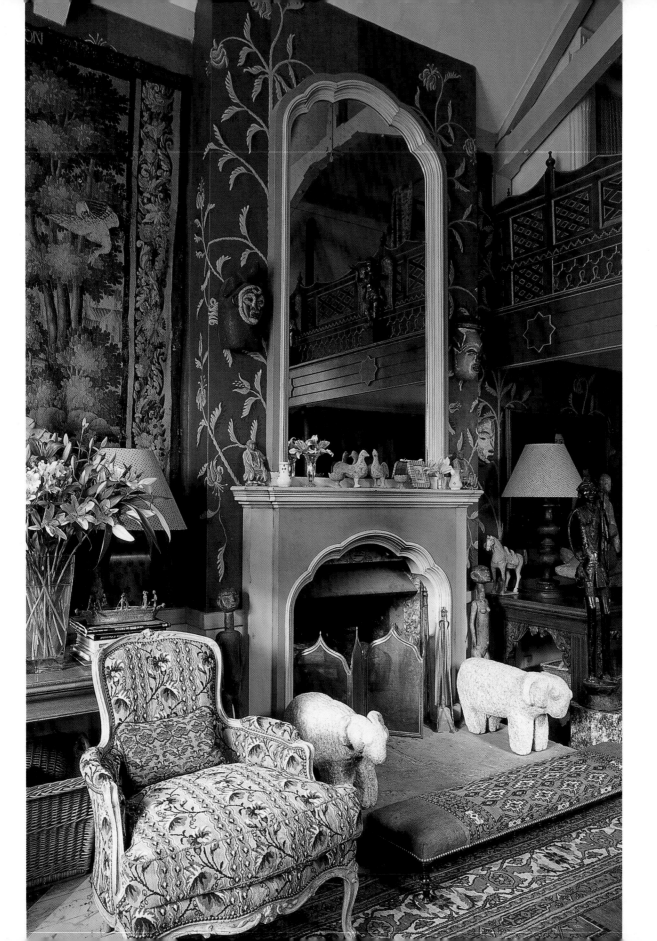

OPPOSITE & ABOVE

In the drawing room the wooden fire surround and the mirror above it were both made to Graham's design.

The walls, painted by Graham in a vibrant over-scaled tree of life design on top of a two-tone vermilion and cherry

stripe, provide a vivid backdrop to an amazingly eclectic collection, from an early eighteenth-century Aubusson

tapestry to African tribal masks. In every corner, and at every level, there is intricate detail: a Japa. se bronze

goose perching on an eighteenth-century Portuguese bracket, a display of Han dynasty horses.

LEFT & OPPOSITE

The outrageous mix of texture, colour and pattern makes the vast drawing room into an Aladdin's cave of treasures. Furniture sits on an antique Persian rug, which in turn covers up a flamboyantly painted trellis-pattern floor. The Gothic-style painted pelmets, sprinkled with gold, echo the vaulting of the ceiling. The modern sofa, comparatively simple in the scale of things, has been upholstered in false suede. The revolving bookcase, which sits to one side, is one of Graham's designs. The exotic style continues upstairs on the mezzanine platform, where a Portuguese walnut bed has been dressed with a bedspread of intricate Uzbekistan needlework.

OPPOSITE

From the yellow-painted hall, there's a view through the master bedroom, to the bathroom beyond. The hall console table, which is nineteenth-century Italian, is inlaid with ivory. To the left of the doorway hangs a pair of Angolan tribal masks.

ABOVE & RIGHT

In the bathroom, walls have been painted an enticing burnt orange, and are hung with Burmese religious scrolls. The curvaceous metal bath is French nineteenth century. The master bedroom is a riot of pattern, with walls battened in blue and white Kashmiri crewelwork, also used for the bed-hangings. The portrait of a man, just glimpsed on the left, is one of a pair of Swedish paintings with painted frames, bought by Graham in a Paris flea market.

LEFT, ABOVE & OPPOSITE

Small and secret, the garden surrounding the school house is laid out as a series of cobbled paths, each lined with low, clipped box. Designed from scratch by Graham, it was planned to fill the area once dominated by the old school playground. On the path leading from the front door to the side entrance, cobbles have been laid in a decorative series of circles, to create interest, and to maintain the Victorian mood. The Chinese stone wild boar is one of a number of statues dotted at random among the small garden's yew trees, Portugues laurels and clipped box.

Norfolk

GEORGIAN GARDENER'S HOUSE

Two miles south of the vast stretch of Holkham beach and nature reserve, in north Norfolk, stands Holkham Hall. Built between 1734 and 1764 by Thomas Coke, the first Earl of Leicester, the house remains in private hands and is the home of the Earl and Countess of Leicester. Yet while the attention of the annual stream of visitors to Holkham is focused on the Hall's breathtaking Palladian architecture, those who live and work on the estate know there are other fine Georgian buildings here to enjoy. Garden House, built for Holkham Hall's head gardener in around 1785 and today the home of Timothy Leese, is surely one of the best.

Given its splendid setting 'slap bang in the middle of 3000 acres [1200 ha]' as Timothy succinctly puts it, here is a house that is best appreciated by approaching on foot. Walking towards it from the south on an early summer's morning you will cross half parkland and half ploughland, then finally across lawns unimpeded by bushes or trees. The original house is perfectly symmetrical, with its garden door flanked by low-silled, wide sash windows. To the west, there is an extra wing, added in the 1880s, to house a new kitchen and additional bedrooms and bathrooms. Stand with your back to the house, and there isn't a single habitation to be spotted in the low-lying Norfolk landscape. 'The location is lonely or tranquil, depending on mood,' says Timothy, 'but that's half the point of its setting.'

Skirt around the side of house, to the north side, and you discover the other key reason for its location. Here, surrounded by thick garden walls, lie the 2.5 ha (6 acres) of Holkham's original kitchen garden, together with its many propagating glasshouses and assorted outbuildings. There's also a fine, original orangery. In the late eighteenth century, this cluster was at the heart of catering on the estate. Today, the kitchen garden is the site for Holkham Gardens Nursery, set up in the 1960s, and now a well-stocked source for hardy ornamental nursery plants. It's nicely fitting, then, that Timothy Leese

- who has owned the nursery for the past seven years - strolls the five-minute walk to the gardens every day, just as the head gardener would once have done.

The house, appropriately called Garden House, was built by Samuel Wyatt (1737-1807), a popular architect and engineer at the time, famously associated with two large houses across the other side of the country: Tatton Park in Cheshire and Shugborough in Staffordshire. He worked on a number of projects at Holkham Hall between 1780 and 1807, and his first commission there was to design and construct the orangery, the kitchen gardens and the head gardener's house nearby. Timothy points out that this would not have been a house to be trifled with. With around fifty staff beneath him, the head gardener was expected to live in some style, and warranted a home of good proportions. With its front and back staircases and entrances, laundry and cellar, servant's bedroom and linen room, as well as spacious reception rooms, it was designed along the lines of a grand country house, but on a much smaller scale.

Garden House certainly has a pleasing exterior, constructed from the same honey-coloured bricks as the main house - not surprising, given that the Hall had its own brickworks. The roof is slate, and Tim recalls hearing that Samuel Wyatt - whose godson was the land agent for Lord Penrhyn (from whose land the slate was mined) - was a keen fan of the material, so

he was clearly looking after kith and kin. As for the orientation of the building, Tim points out that it's an intriguing five degrees off due north on the compass point. 'It's thought that a bothy, to house some of the gardeners, was already on the site, so rather than knock it down, the house was built a little off-centre,' he says.

What is particularly interesting is that, given its two main entrances, front and back, it's hard to discern which one was originally the more important. The north door is closer to the kitchen garden, and once had a driveway directly in front. (Tim has now rerouted this, as nursery customers tended to wander down it, then press their faces to his windows.) However, from the garden entrance the hall leads into the principal reception rooms - the drawing room is to the right, the dining room to the left. There is no evidence, Tim says, that a driveway ever swept around to this side of the house. The layout, then, is a triumph. 'There are no cars on a drive to impede my views of the countryside,' says Tim. And there would never have been any carriages, either.

RIGHT   *Wisteria-clad Garden House was built by Samuel Wyatt around 1785 for the head gardener of Holkham Hall. Legend has it that the mature holly-leafed oaks around the house grew from seeds that came over from Italy, contained in the packing cases used to protect statues and paintings for the new Hall.*

Take a tour around the house as it is today, and the layout within is as regular and well-planned as its perfect exterior. Given its Grade II* listing, major alterations would have been out of the question, but Timothy found little that he needed to change. Enter through the garden door, past the staircase and principal rooms, and to the right there is a study and downstairs cloakroom, and to the left, the 'book room', which leads directly into the kitchen. In order to maximize light from an east-facing window in the study, Timothy's architect, Robert Chance, aligned all the doors, so it's possible to stand in the kitchen and see straight through to the garden. A similar alignment took place upstairs, and a wall was removed on the landing. Now sunlight floods in from the sash window directly above the garden door.

It is the windows, Tim says, that are the best feature of the house. They are wide, and low, though never out of proportion, and because all the principal rooms face south, you pass from one sunny room to

LEFT *The south-facing garden entrance looks out on to uninterrupted parkland, part of the Hall's vast park. Above the semi-glazed door is a decorative fanlight, featuring the Prince of Wales feathered crest. The honey-coloured brickwork of the house is identical to the bricks used for Holkham Hall – no coincidence, as both came from Holkham's own brickworks. Simple table and chairs make this quiet spot a pleasant place for Timothy to to sit and relax.*

the next. Even the garden entrance has a fanlight (featuring the Prince of Wales feathered crest) and glazed side panels. Yet look at a floor plan and good circulation is also key. The kitchen alone has five doors; all, on inspection, are necessary. One leads to the dining room, one to the lobby (and back door), one to the larder, one to the laundry, and the last is the entrance point from the book room. It may have been built in the 1880s, but here is an immaculately planned kitchen; situated to one side of the main building, but nevertheless functioning at its heart.

Upstairs, the layout has evolved considerably since the nineteenth-century extension. When the house was originally built, it would have had two principal bedrooms, immediately above the dining room and drawing room, facing south, and two further bedrooms on the north side. With the late nineteenth-century addition (which has a staircase leading from the kitchen to an upstairs lobby and linen cupboard) the owners would have embraced the fashion for plumbed bathrooms. Today, there are four bedrooms and three bathrooms – and the original linen cupboard still survives.

As for the architecture within, it is satisfyingly intact, although when Timothy first took possession some of the ceilings and floorboards had rotted and had to be replaced. In keeping with many modest Georgian houses, the style is not elaborate:

wainscotting and dado rails are scaled down, and there are no cornices in the bedrooms. But Timothy points out that Samuel Wyatt was a geometric designer, with a tendency to plain detailing. Yet it is a simplicity imbued with elegance, evident in the sweep of the wooden stair-rail, the arched fireplace alcoves in both drawing room and dining room, and the gentle arch of the glazed garden door.

Happily, Timothy has resisted the temptation to fill all alcoves with shelves and cupboards: those in the

ABOVE & RIGHT *The house has two front doors: here, the main staircase is viewed from the garden entrance. On the nineteenth-century white-painted console sits a pair of new Korean double gourds, reflected in an antique gilded mirror bought at Christie's. The garden door looks directly on to parkland, with a stand of beech, oak and Scots pine. The park would have been designed partly with shooting in mind, so the trees provide cover for pheasant and partridge.*

drawing room still hold freestanding furniture, as they would most certainly always have done. In the dining room, he blocked up a doorway which had been inserted into the right-hand alcove, and simply added display shelving and cupboards below. In the book room, architect Robert Chance was responsible for lining the walls with bookshelves, to house Timothy's huge personal collection, and for inserting a concealed door. While the fireplaces are original, downstairs Timothy replaced inappropriate 'new' slips, inserted by the previous owner, with plain stone ones copied from upstairs. He also reinstated the open hearths, and fires frequently blaze in every room.

It is pleasing to see that, rather than over-clutter the rooms with furniture and paintings, Timothy has decorated with a light touch, so that attention is thrown back to the views beyond the windows. Walls throughout are in pale or dark tones of a neutral grey-green (according to whether the room faces north or south), flooring is coir matting (except for terracotta tiles in the hall) and upholstery neutral. 'The rooms are not really very big, so the spaces seem more restful if they are all much the same shade,' comments Timothy. The subdued lichen colour, he explains, is a complimentary tone that shows off both people and flowers to their best advantage. One hopes that the head gardener, roses in hand, would have sincerely approved.

LEFT

In the dining room, the alcoves either side of the chinmeypiece are used to display a late eighteenth-century Crown Derby dessert service. Symmetrically arranged on the original mantelpiece is a collection of early nineteenth-century Wedgwood drabware, while above it hangs a seventeenth-century print, after a painting by Paul Bril. The romantic landscape is entitled Pan and Syrinx, and the original hangs in The Louvre. The plaster casts to either side are reproductions of Roman statuary at Holkham Hall.

ABOVE

The simple kitchen boasts a traditional Aga for heating and cooking, and plain tongue-and-groove cabinets designed by the architect Robert Chance.

OPPOSITE & ABOVE

In the book room, which links the hall to the kitchen, the walls are lined with bookcases, also designed by Robert Chance.

Above the fireplace hangs an engraving of Het Loo Palace in Holland, bought by Timothy in New York. To either side

hang a pair of Edwardian mirrored sconces. The comfortable furniture is a mix of inherited pieces and antique finds.

The glass-topped Edwardian desk in the window was given to Timothy by a friend, in exchange for a garden design.

OPPOSITE

The principal guest bedroom is dominated by a nineteenth-century painted four-poster bed and a chaise longue, bought by Timothy on a trip to Scotland. Both are upholstered in Colefax & Fowler's classic Bowood chintz.

LEFT & ABOVE

On the original fireplace, there's a collection of treasures: a pair of Edwardian glass candlesticks, typically used as dressing table lights, willow-pattern plates, an ebony apple and a late nineteenth-century glass flower vase. The walls are painted the same gentle, specially mixed shade of grey-green used throughout the house, and the original brass door furniture is still in place.

ABOVE

Tim's bathroom, which was originally a dressing room, has a north-facing view across to Samuel Wyatt's Vinery.

The Edwardian bath has been carefully positioned, so that he can lie in it and look directly out of the window.

The walls are lined with many black and white photographs of friends and family, simply framed.

OPPOSITE

In one of the guest rooms is a 1920s cane and mahogany bed, bought by Tim at an auction in Fakenham.

On the walls are photographs of family, and a pair of Norfolk topographical views.

LEFT, RIGHT & BELOW

The beds of Holkham Gardens Nursery are well stocked with hardy ornamental nursery plants, while some plants are raised in a selection of glass houses close by. The cobbled yard is enclosed by a series of outbuildings built in the 1880s, including a tack room and stable for the head gardener's horse and cart. The original pump and trough had become overgrown with conifers, and were discovered by Timothy only after he had cleared the yard. He designed the stone-topped garden table himself.

Suffolk
TUDOR COUNTRY HOUSE

The English house is not always what it seems. The symmetrical façade of a late Georgian house, with its regular sash windows and smooth plastered walls, may hide a much more complex architectural history. Only after extensive research will it finally reveal its secrets, turning out to be a reflection – over an extended period of time – of local social history. The earlier the building, the greater is the likelihood that a house will be an agglomeration of tastes, styles and family fortunes. Over the centuries, some key features will remain, while others are irretrievably lost.

Such is the case with Charles and Sarah Fenwick's home, set in a valley of outstanding natural beauty. This is the area of Suffolk affectionately known as Constable Country, and the house is even depicted in one of the artist's paintings, nestling between mature trees under a lowering grey East Anglian sky. The house is right at the centre of the village but, unseen behind a yew hedge, feels a little secretive, even though to locals it is as much part of the village's history as its fourteenth-century church.

In the tradition of many country properties, it has been passed down the generations. It was first purchased by Charles's grandmother in 1936, as a replacement for their much larger home, Temple Dinsley. Temple Dinsley had been extended for the family by Sir Edwin Lutyens in 1908, and Lutyens also helped with the 1936 renovation of the Suffolk house. Charles was born and brought up here, but it was only in 1982, when his father died, that he inherited the property as his own. In the late 1990s, he masterminded a total refurbishment of the house and gardens, enlisting the aid of his friend and designer, George Carter. At the same time he married Sarah, and she oversaw the interior design, alongside her son, the interior decorator Willie Nickerson.

Charles is knowledgeable on the house and points out its long history, stretching back six hundred years. The site is older still – there are known to be Roman villa foundations here, on top of which a Saxon house was built. But it wasn't until the fifteenth century that the timber framework of the existing building was erected, by a Catholic family of nearby Gifford's Hall. The Mannocks were sheep farmers and landowners who had prospered from the thriving Suffolk wool trade. In the sixteenth century, they added a first-floor solar chamber, whose decorative wall paintings are still intact today (the owners now call this the Requiem Room). The family continued to live at the hall until, after the collapse of the wool trade and as a result of their adherence to the Catholic faith, they lost much of their fortune.

In the late eighteenth century, when the Napoleonic wars saw a resurgence in the corn trade in Suffolk, local fortunes changed again. In 1795, relations of the original Mannocks brought the house up to date by cloaking the Tudor building in a plastered façade and adding bow windows.

It is this version of the house that is recognizable today. Inside, the shell of the Tudor hall house (which would once have been divided into a dining hall, parlour, scullery and buttery) was substantially remodelled. The Georgian owners added an elegant new oval entrance hall with three arches. Through the left one, you pass into a panelled dining room, and to the right, into a papyrus yellow drawing room, with windows looking south and west. Straight ahead is the double-height entrance hall, with a sweeping staircase and triple arches, added by Sir Edwin Lutyens.

Scrutinize aerial photographs of the house today, plus older family photographs taken during the 1936 renovation, and you see that this main building isn't the whole story. In fact, the house is arranged right around a courtyard garden. Stretching along the north side is what the Fenwicks term the 'service wing', which now houses the kitchen where the dairy would have been. To the east, parallel to the Tudor building, is a rectangular, two-storey grain store, built in 1810 as the owners continued to thrive. Linking this to the main house is a seventeenth-century building housing a small hall and a library. The library's Gothic bay window was an 1860 addition.

It's never easy to blend architectural styles, and when Charles decided to renovate the grain store to provide more relaxed weekend accommodation for just the two of them he called in a number of local architects. It was George Carter's design that proved most appropriate. He drew up plans for a simple east-facing façade, with eight symmetrically placed sash windows, and double doors, beneath an over-scaled Gibbsian portico, leading out into the gardens. The result blends sympathetically with the slightly more formal Georgian façade at the front, and is painted a specially mixed off-white. The same colour was used on the clapboard of the service wing.

The central portion of the converted grain store forms the yellow-painted Garden Room, with wide

OPPOSITE *The west façade's Georgian bow windows, one fronting the drawing room, the other the dining room, retain their curved eighteenth-century glass and, inside, the original shutter housing.*

French doors leading to a series of formal gardens, and the parkland beyond. To one side, is Charles's writing room. The master bedroom upstairs is huge, and was deliberately designed to create a tranquil, loft-like mood. Charles points out the high ceiling beams. 'We know these were recycled from the fifteenth-century hall,' he explains. 'Some beams show traces of the decorative wall painting in the Requiem Room.'

Sarah, who owns Myriad Antiques in London, is responsible for the majority of the lovely antiques at the house. She has found many of the major pieces - such as the 1810 dining table and the French nineteenth-century pressed glass chandelier in the dining room - as well as decorative items, including antique French nuns' linen sheets that drape the four-poster bed in the master bedroom. Other heirlooms have more personal significance. In the Chinoiserie Room is the 1920 Heal's bed in which Charles was born. The striped sofa in the drawing room was originally bought for Temple Dinsley, and the fabric, uncovered beneath layers of upholstery, is the original Howard sofa underlay.

Charles created The Chelsea Gardener, and has therefore had a major hand in the garden design. When renovations began, he bulldozed the grounds (in the early twentieth century, much of the surrounding land had been agricultural). Then, with the help of George Carter, he added a series of formal gardens, including a rose garden to the south, and a kitchen garden that can be seen from the kitchen windows.

Looking east from the master bedroom windows, the view in high summer is of a tapestry of 50,000 bedding plants in full bloom. As part of his business, Charles develops and tests new seed varieties. Even the tiny courtyard garden is planted up with sweet-smelling plumbago and olive trees in vast copper pots.

As you wander around the house it's clear that furniture and decorative accessories have been carefully chosen to reflect the varying historical periods of the house. Yet the Fenwicks have also been wise, perhaps, to choose contrasting looks for each room. The walls of the Garden Room are hung with paintings by twentieth-century artists, such as the Suffolk-based Cecil Lay and Gwyneth Johnson. Furniture is plain and simple, as is the wooden mantelpiece, designed and made by George Carter. In the White Bedroom, with its original Georgian panelling, are twin Spanish beds, dated around 1910,

and pretty *toile de Jouy*. The *en suite* bathroom is built into what was once an adjoining powder room.

In the kitchen is a more intriguing mix of periods and styles. The subdued linoleum floor, although new, is are very similar to the tiles laid by Charles's grandmother. The kitchen table, on the other hand, originates from a French château in Burgundy; dated 1530, it feels very appropriate for the Tudor period of the house. Charles points out that the Aga has been doing service since the 1930s. 'And,' he adds, 'the fridge was bought in 1953, to hold champagne for the Coronation!' It is also still in fine working order.

Houses evolve over the centuries, and the Fenwicks continue to make improvements to theirs. A new stable block has just been completed, and in the cellar a Catholic chapel is in progress, an addition that the Mannocks would no doubt have approved. But perhaps what makes this house such a delight is the Fenwicks' relaxed approach to it. 'It's not a precious house,' Sarah concludes. 'Children visit here and they roar around, and straight away feel very happy.' Which is exactly how the best English houses should feel.

ABOVE & RIGHT *This part of the garden is planted up with sweet-scented lavender beds, interspersed with a mix of garden objects old and new. The Gothic library bay window was inserted in 1860, although this part of the building is a seventeenth-century addition.*

OPPOSITE & ABOVE

Arches are a recurrent theme in the imposing hall. Echoing a trio of Georgian arches, which lead off the oval entrance,

three more appear to the right of the staircase. Sir Edwin Lutyens added this elegant feature, as part of his refurbishment

in the 1930s. Close to the stairs stands a seventeenth-century table, decorated with unusual hunting flasks from the

turn of the last century, and a pair of painted wooden finials. The view, through the oval entrance, is to the dining room.

The hall walls are hung with a large collection of first impression portrait prints, amassed by Charles's grandfather.

ABOVE & RIGHT

The formal dining room is set for dinner with the Fenwicks' family porcelain. Charles had the eighteenth-century originals, bearing a phoenix (the family crest). copied in the 1970s, while he was in Hong Kong. The pretty fireplace was installed in 1936 by Charles's grandmother, and the contemporary columns either side were designed by George Carter. Hanging over the table is a French nineteenth century pressed glass chandelier. The panelling in the room is original to the Georgian refurbishment, and has been painted a soft squashed tomato colour. On one wall hangs a portrait of a French maréchal, flanked by a pair of eighteenth-century gilded mirrors.

ABOVE

In the Garden Room, walls are painted a cheerful sunny
yellow and the furniture has been chosen for comfort.
The painting above the simple mahogany cupboard depicts
a 1950s East Anglian scene. Just beyond, the hall (in the
south-facing seventeenth-century addition) is papered
in a Sanderson William Morris wallpaper.

RIGHT

The drawing room's walls are hung with paintings
of birds and landscapes acquired in Udaipur, India.
The imposing Gothic desk is dated 1780, and the black
lacquer console is also an eighteenth-century piece.

ABOVE

The kitchen is situated in the fifteenth-century north service wing, where early lead mullion windows still survive. Many of the kitchen cabinets and fittings, including the wooden drainer and worktop, are as they were when the house was refurbished in 1936. The Aga dates from the same period. The old butcher sign hanging above it is part of a collection acquired locally by Charles.

OPPOSITE

The sixteenth-century timber table, surrounded by simple English country chairs, is the perfect place for sociable family gatherings. Overhead, modern metal-shaded French lights hang from the low beams. The chunky painted wooden candlesticks probably originated from a church.

LEFT & ABOVE

The Gothic-style glazed back door leads out into the kitchen garden (the kitchen window can be seen to the right in the photograph opposite), and either side of the door stands a pair of terracotta obelisks from The Chelsea Gardener. The rustic clapboard on the exterior walls, which was probably added in the eighteenth century, is today softened by a trailing hop. From the side door, the view is to the south, across mown grass, towards the village church.

ABOVE & RIGHT

The view south, framed by a metal gate made to George Carter's design, looks the length of a broad mown path called the wild flower walk, as it is fringed to either side with fields of wild flowers. Beyond, there is a 'wiggly walk', which leads through the park. Some of the many bedding plants, grown for Charles's breeding performance trials, can be seen from the Fenwicks' bedroom window. The mature parkland trees beyond are thought to have been planted in 1820.

GEORGIAN SCHOOL HOUSE

On clear-skied days, Elizabeth Gage is told, aircraft regularly use her home to get their north-south bearings. It's easy to see why. The converted School House is something of a landmark even at ground level, with its tower fashioned like a Greek basilica and distinctive trios of arched windows flanking every one of its four wings. Yet it's not until Elizabeth points it out (or you're flying at 10,000 m or 30,000 ft) that you realize the Bath stone building forms a perfect cross. Look at it on plan, and it's possible to see that the drawing room - which forms the long arm of the cross outline - points due south. What might its architect have thought had he known that the cruciform shape he conceived on paper is now on daily 3-D view from above?

The pilots may be none the wiser as to why the house is cross-shaped, but Elizabeth is fully informed. The original school house, completed in 1824, was funded by the village church, so it's no wonder that its architect, Robert Abrahams, chose a religious theme. From the 1820s onwards, all things Gothic had become almost as much a favourite as the Classical style, so in keeping with the prevailing fashion there are pointed arched windows overlaid with ornate stone tracery, and arched double entrance doors to match. There are also decorative crucifixes on the tower. Precisely because of its characteristic arches and insistence on accuracy, Gothic was a look particularly popular for churches and other buildings with ecclesiastical links.

When a building has been converted from one use to another, it's always a test to see if the space (not to mention the architectural features) works, however lovely it looks. For this Georgian school house, the transformation is seamless. It helped that the older children's school room had long ago been extended (in 1854), so the south-facing drawing room already had suitably lofty proportions. Those big Gothic windows, to aid study, also now conveniently flood the house with light. But most importantly, the four wings - which once provided separate classrooms for a span of ages - now provide companionable, yet private, accommodation. 'There can be just one person in the drawing room, or twenty in the dining room,' says Elizabeth, 'and it's always cosy, and no one ever feels lost.'

The School House has been Elizabeth's weekend home for thirteen years. She is only the third domestic occupant since Robert Kime (who, more recently, was responsible for refashioning the interior of Clarence House for Prince Charles) first converted it in 1967. Unlike the rash of city developments up and down the country, which have randomly chopped up old primary schools into one- or two-bedroom flats, this conversion has been done with sensitivity and flair. Long before Elizabeth purchased it, all the appropriate domestic heating, lighting and plumbing had been installed, and rooms haven't been partitioned off. Her living accommodation sprawls comfortably across the ground floor, with three guest bedrooms and a bathroom upstairs. The tower is purely decorative, accessible only from outside.

The English have long been fans of the rural bolt-hole, to which they can escape after the city's working week, and Elizabeth, a London-based jewellery designer, is no exception. Born 'within hearing of Bow bells' (and so, technically, a London cockney), but brought up in America, she found herself longing for a tranquil spot within two hours' drive of London. Every week she scoured the pages of *Country Life* in vain. 'Everything I saw was either too big, too expensive, or too far away,' she remembers. And

then her luck turned; the last issue she planned to take carried The School House. Not only did it meet all her criteria (intimate, affordable, accessible) but it looked 'a beautiful place'. She viewed it on a Thursday, and bought it the following Monday. 'The atmosphere was just what I wanted,' she says. 'I fell in love with it.'

Ask her why, and she says she feels 'enveloped' by the house. This makes sense, because although each wing holds a single room - drawing room, study, kitchen and her bedroom respectively - she travels constantly back and forth through the central zone. Originally, this middle section held the headmaster's study (now the dining room), a beady-eyed location if ever there was one. Cleverly, the hall is now divided into two, so there are no longer open views into Elizabeth's private quarters. Instead, the main entrance leads into a long, narrow hall, looking through to the drawing room, while Elizabeth's bedroom is off a smaller, intimately tented hall.

If the house itself doesn't fit a traditional domestic template, neither does the garden. A keen gardener, Elizabeth values the quirkiness of the house being right in the middle of it's land. Between each projecting wing of the building, contrasting plants and

OPPOSITE *Original double Gothic doors lead into the secondary hall. Elizabeth inherited the stone urns with the house, while the iron chairs, with their nautilus-pattern backs, are modern American. The diminutive arched windows above belong to a guest bedroom.*

vegetation grow, and a different mood unravels. Elizabeth has constantly added to and replanted the original beds, so that the boundaries between indoors and outdoors blur. From her drawing room, one window overlooks the rose garden, and another her *potager*, or vegetable garden, with radishes, lettuces and beetroot in neat rows beneath the crab apples. From the kitchen, there are views to a raised garden, and from her bedroom, to vines and a vine house. Beyond the clipped parterre lawns near the house extends an enchanting wild garden.

Inside, that same theme of contrast and balance, is played out in each room. Less imaginative owners might have struggled to visually knit together a series of ground-floor rooms radiating from two separate halls. But with her design background, and an obsession with creating lovely homes (she has moved fifteen times), Elizabeth has succeeded in creating a dramatic interior. 'I wanted to put together something that was joyous and cosy,' she comments. Her decorative palette, consequently, is not for shrinking violets. Those original church benefactors might have balked at the rich marmalade walls in the drawing room, or the dark wine of the dining room, not to mention the dress fabrics gathered abundantly at the windows, but it's a look wholly worthy of the extravagant architecture outside.

That the patterns Elizabeth has chosen have

personal significance makes for an even more interesting mix. In the drawing room, giant hand-painted oak leaves sprawl above the picture rail. 'These feel very English, and they are a symbol of strength and friendship,' she comments. In her bedroom, the fanciful bed canopy is covered with painted roses, executed by artist Graham Carr. (Outdoors, roses are a recurrent theme, lovingly grown by Elizabeth through vegetables, or in the wild garden, as well as in the rose garden itself.) A black and white screen in the study has a particularly personal resonance. It was a present from the artist Maddy Benard and depicts a Regency scene (enlarged from a writing blotter cover) featuring Elizabeth's own childhood home in Shropshire.

Given that Elizabeth set about decorating her weekend home on a restrained budget, it also suited her that minimal structural alterations were required. The drawing room needed the most work. The previous owners had installed a mezzanine floor, which they used as a study area. Elizabeth took this down, and at the same time uncovered one of the three Gothic windows, which had been slated over from inside. Why, you wonder, would the builders have gone to the trouble of blacking out such a dramatic

LEFT & ABOVE *The paved area between the east side of the drawing room and the kitchen forms the perfect spot for eating outdoors in summer. The beds below the kitchen window are planted with hostas and white enenomes. Elaborate Gothic stone finials rise above each window.*

window? 'I have been told that each room had its own pot-bellied stove,' says Elizabeth. 'It's thought the pipes were routed across one of the windows, so it was necessary to cover up the glass.'

The interior complete, Elizabeth, has ploughed her time and energy into creating a whimsical and welcoming garden. It was she who first planted the *potager*, a French style ornamental kitchen garden, and she completely redesigned the original rose garden. 'Over time the whole vista from the drawing room completely changed,' she remarks. Between the house and the rose garden there are now neat borders of box and lavender. In the wild garden, which she loves for its many varied greens, she chose a fallen apple tree (which, still rooted, provides her with cooking apples) as the main focus for the design. Throughout the project she has worked hand-in-hand with interior and garden designer Graham Carr.

What does she consider to be the true English core of the house? 'I love the Gothic quality of it,' she says, in barely perceptible mid-Atlantic tones. 'It's so nearly a folly - but it's not, because it is so light, and welcoming, and easy to live in.'

ABOVE & OPPOSITE

The 'sun gate', designed by Elizabeth Gage, links an avenue of lime trees with the formal

garden at the south-west side of the house. To the right can be seen one of the drawing

room windows, and, to the left, the study window. The formal garden is a mix of clipped

box and lavender borders, puncutated with ivy trained and clipped into large spheres.

Behind it lies the rose garden.

LEFT & ABOVE

The main entrance hall is decorated in the red tones that Elizabeth Gage loves, with curtains made from orange dress material. The wallpaper, now discontinued, was from Scarisbrook & Baite. Many favourite treasures are collected in this room. The Jacobean side table is an inherited piece, and on the floor is a tiger-design rug by contemporary rug designer Phoebe Hart. The drawing room still has the original iron window furniture.

ABOVE & RIGHT

In the study, there is a mix of highly decorative pieces. The antique bureau was repainted for Elizabeth by Jeffrey Pick, and in front of it sits a Gothic-style chair by Graham Carr. The bureau is surrounded by twentieth-century paintings of St Paul de Vence, by Elizabeth's grandmother while on the Côte d'Azur. In the sitting area, there is a comfortable 1950s sofa and a modern coffee table brought from America. The black cabinet painted with flowers was also designed by Graham Carr. On it sits a contemporary sculpture bought in Spain, and a figure from Santa Fe. The elaborate gilded lamps either side of the sofa come from Peru.

ABOVE

The drawing room is all-enveloping, with its marmalade-painted walls and yellow silk dress fabric curtains. Graham Carr hand-painted the floor, as well as the giant oak-leaf frieze and the decorative wreath above the door. Dominating one wall is a seventeenth-century English tapestry, while in front of the sofa sits a 1920s mirrored coffee table that belonged to Elizabeth's grandmother.

RIGHT

The wooden fireplace surround is new, and was designed and painted by Graham Carr. The fine Eurpean gilded mirror above it was a present to Elizabeth from her husband.

LEFT & ABOVE

Hung dramatically at each end of the drawing room is a pair of mid nineteenth-century chandeliers. Elizabeth has chosen large-scale furniture and accessories, to balance the expansive proportions of the room, which was once the older children's school room. At each end sits a large sofa: one originally bought in America, and the other made in England. There are one-off, special pieces of furniture, too. The ceramic 'throne' is by the contemporary ceramicist Emma Lush.

OPPOSITE

Starman Dancing, the painting hanging above a console table designed by Graham Carr, is by Elizabeth's mother.

OPPOSITE & ABOVE

The small and intimate tented hall, with walls and ceiling covered in a pretty green toile de Jouy, links the kitchen and master bedroom to the main entrance hall. In here, the furniture is elegant and scaled down, to match the hall's proportions. The Swedish painted clock is eighteenth-century and the central table French Directoire. The master bedroom is dominated by the elaborate 'flower bed', designed and painted by Graham Carr. Beyond it, in the corner, is a walnut chest of drawers inherited from Elizabeth's uncle. The flower painting hanging above it, dated 1919, was painted by her grandmother.

LEFT & ABOVE

The formal areas of Elizabeth's garden are green and peaceful places. A side garden, symmetrically planted with lime trees and decorative box balls, has as its focus a concrete sunray sculpture. In the rose garden, which can be seen directly from the drawing room, box-edged beds hold tall rose bushes and trained fruit trees, which are shielded from winds by a high box hedge.

ABOVE & RIGHT

*Her wild garden, with its many mature trees and even
a Victorian folly, is a favourite tranquil spot for Elizabeth.
Part of the garden is dominated by a vast apple tree – still
growing and bearing fruit, despite having long since been
blown over in a storm. At the very end of the garden,
half-hidden, is a stone statue by contemporary sculptor
Judith Verity, depicting the figure of a lady.*

PALLADIAN FOLLY

At the height of the English love affair with Palladian architecture, eighteenth-century architects, it seems, were just as tempted by the notion of the small but perfectly designed building as by a commission for the grand country mansion. Up and down the country, it was the heyday of the folly: towers and classical ruins there had been aplenty, but now miniature Palladian villas began to dot the landscape. In the grounds of Tendring Hall in Suffolk, another beautiful example was being added to the tally. Over two and a half centuries later, it still stands in breathtaking surroundings, looking as immaculate - and perfectly proportioned - as ever.

The Temple of the Four Seasons, more affectionately known as the Fishing Temple, or even just 'the Temple', is today leased from Tendring Hall by interior designer Veere Grenney. He took on this graceful and charming garden building twenty years ago, and in that time has upgraded and added to the accommodation, so that it has become the perfect urban dweller's retreat. Arriving for the weekend on a Friday evening, Veere can park his car on the drive, then take the short stroll through the formal box and yew hedges, rose gardens and lawns to reach the front door, which is tucked to the right of the arched undercroft entrance. On a summer's evening, with the lime trees reflected in the mirror-like water of the canal, the folly is, Veere comments, 'the most peaceful place on earth'.

He should know. Veere was born in New Zealand and travelled the world before settling and working in England. Given the grandness of his clients, and the important historical properties he designs for, it is no surprise he sought out the Temple for his own, although he is not the first designer to enjoy its physical perfection. David Hicks lived here from the mid 1950s to the early 60s, and it was Hicks, Veere says, who saved the building from impending decrepitude. Hicks installed basic plumbing and lighting, and added a bathroom and kitchen downstairs. In those days, the main room was painted in Chinese yellow, with blue and white furnishings, and Country Life ran a feature on it. Today, with its shell pink walls, it has become a subtler incarnation.

Many well-known architects of the day indulged in folly building, and for a long time it was unclear who was responsible for Tendring's bucolic folly. However, Veere has pieced together information from scholars at The Georgian Society and English Heritage, to conclude that the English architect Sir Robert Taylor (1714-88) designed and built the folly, which is remarkably similar in style to two Palladian-style villas attributed to Taylor. Long after the garden designer Sir Humphry Repton was commissioned in 1780 to design formal gardens within the park, the folly continued to stand on its fringes, a 'pleasure pavilion for country pursuits'.

These days it is far from ignored, and is Grade I listed. Ask Veere what most pleases him about the building, and he returns, time and again, to the perfection of its setting. The folly is planted facing due east, with the grand floor-to-ceiling window of the upstairs drawing room looking straight down the canal. To the back of the folly, facing west and capturing every sunset, you look out straight across Suffolk meadowland. 'Because it is so placed, the light is absolutely perfect, more so because it reflects from the water,' Veere comments. And at night,

in winter, he can lie on the sofa in the window and watch the moon rise in the east, hanging big and low, 'hauntingly beautiful'.

But the star attraction is the classical perfection of the building, inside and out. Even at a distance, the silhouette is well balanced, with an identical 'shoulder' to left and right, and a characteristic Palladian portico above the central window. Inside, it is what was once termed the saloon, the first-floor room 9 m (30 ft) long, that demands attention. Even on a dull day it is flooded with light, and it has retained all its original features. Its lofty, elaborately moulded stucco ceiling features four figures, representing the four seasons. Symmetrically placed at each end of the room are plaster busts of Roman emperors, depicting the four ages of man. And then, at either side of the east-facing window, there are two alcoves, which may once have held statues of a shepherd and shepherdess, or possibly Adam and Eve.

It is this room, ultimately, that is the whole point of the building. The folly was built, Veere says, as a

RIGHT *Fringing both sides of the long canal are avenues of lime trees. These were planted to replace the 250-year-old sweet chestnuts that had lined the canal since it was built in the mid eighteenth century. Storms and time had destroyed many of the trees, so new lime trees were planted in their place. The canal, filled with carp, is the perfect location for a spot of weekend fishing.*

ABOVE

Today the villa is still painted in an authentic ochre, faithful to the warm tones of the original Italian Palladian villas. One of the grand floor-to-ceiling windows looks straight down the canal, while to the back of the folly, facing west, there is an uninterrupted view of meadowland.

OPPOSITE

A pair of simple wooden posts, with an eighteenth-century statue of a shepherd just beyond, direct the visitor round, past the box hedge, straight to the front door.

pleasure pavilion for the landed gentry, just a short stroll from the main house and a place to come, take tea, and watch country pursuits. Relaxing in the first-floor saloon, eighteenth-century gentlemen might have watched others fishing in the canal in one direction, or enjoyed the sight of coursing dogs and hares flitting across the autumnal landscape in the other. Other facilities were minimal. In the right 'shoulder', on the ground floor, there would have been a scullery with an open fire, for making refreshments. The left wing would have lain empty, or used as a store, built purely to maintain the balanced proportions of the exterior.

Today, the decorative scheme is contemporary, although over the last two decades Veere has also decorated it, like Hicks, with Chinese yellow and blue and white, and more recently, in shocking pink (for which it was photographed for *Architectural Digest*). The rough Suffolk hand-woven mediaeval matting on the floor contrasts with the satin curtains that, in the classic mid eighteenth-century 'pull up' style, festoon the tops of the windows. The furniture is a confident clash of periods, in Veere's trademark style: a retro 1949 floor lamp is teamed with an original 1810 *Directoire* chair and a decorative chandelier.

To the casual observer, what most captures the attention is the elaborate stucco on the ceiling and on the chimneypiece. Given that by the 1950s the place

was in disrepair, how much restoration work has been required? Veere says that, long before his time, the ceiling had been boarded up for many years, thus preserving the stucco. And David Hicks had also played his part. What would have been the original marble mantelpiece had long since been ripped out, although the plasterwork chimneypiece above was confirmed as original. Below it, David Hicks installed a carved wood surround, appropriate to the building.

What Veere has added to, over the years, are the rooms that have turned the folly from a classic English eccentricity into a comfortable weekend retreat. The entire place was rewired and replumbed. Then he installed a new bathroom on the ground floor in the left 'shoulder', to add to the bedroom Hicks had built in, with French doors leading out to the side. A new kitchen and dining room stand in the central block, with the staircase to the right. Most recently, he has restored the old dog kennels, five minutes' walk across the grounds, converting them into a detached guest wing by adding a further two bedrooms and two bathrooms.

While most of Hicks' original fittings have been removed, one legacy remains. It was he who in 1960 commissioned the architect Raymond Erith to insert an oval *oeil de boeuf* window directly below the east-facing drawing room window. Now it affords fabulous views of the canal directly from the dining room.

RIGHT *With its exaggerated pediment, extended eaves, and arched undercroft entrance below, The folly is a perfect scaled-down version of the many Palladian-style villas that once dotted the Italian landscape. It was built as a haven where the landed gentry could take tea and watch country pursuits, and today the beauty of its simplicity and symmetry are protected by a Grade I listing.*

Respectful of the synergy between the folly and its surroundings, Veere has also done much work on the gardens and the canal. When it was first dug and filled, in the middle of the eighteenth century, the waterway was lined by sweet chestnut trees, but by the time Veere took over the property, the canal was in a state of disrepair, and many of the trees were later lost in the great storm that swept across southern and eastern England in autumn 1987. In tandem with the owners of the Tendring Hall estate, he has had the canal drained and rerevetted, and planted the lime trees that now fringe the water. Veere's rowing boat sits ready for use outside the pavilion, along with a pair of kayaks, and he often goes fishing. The canal is fed by running water from a stream at one end, and itself flows into Repton's lake in the park grounds, which is filled with carp. The formal gardens have also been relandscaped, with box and yew trees, to look much as they would have done in the eighteenth century.

It may be twenty years since he took on this marvellous slice of architectural history, but it is a love affair that started even longer ago than that. 'I first saw the Temple in a book on David Hicks, when I was fourteen, and loved it,' Veere says. 'In a sense, this has always been my house.'

ABOVE & RIGHT

The grand saloon on the upper floor features the original elaborately moulded stucco
ceiling, and Veere Greeney has furnished the room in his own inimitable and elegant
style. A copy of a 1950s armchair in pink cotton is teamed with a Queen Anne chair
upholstered in a white linen sheet. In the corner stands a William IV rosewood library
table. The dramatic, late nineteenth-century chandelier is Venetian, while the 1949
floor lamp is by Gino Safatti for Arteluce.

OPPOSITE & ABOVE

The bedrooms have been decorated with a light, pretty touch. In the guest bedroom the painted wood four-poster bed was designed by Veere Grenney, and is hung with pink and white striped cotton. At the foot of the bed sits an eighteenth-century painted Italian table. In Veere's bedroom, there are French doors which open directly on to the canal. Throughout the folly, the floors are covered with Suffolk hand-woven mediaeval matting. The original staircase leads directly up to the saloon. The walls are hung with a series of pressed ferns, dated 1916, from New Zealand, to remind Veere Grenney of his antipodean roots.

LEFT & ABOVE

David Hicks commissioned the oeil de boeuf *window from Raymond Erith to give a spectacular framed view eastward straight down the canal. With its director chairs set on the sunny porch, this makes a tranquil early morning spot to sit and relax.*

OVERLEAF

A fishing boat, drawn up to the edge of the canal, sits ready for that most traditional of English country pursuits – fishing. There are also a couple of kayaks close by.

HOME FARM HOUSE

Planted, like the most perfect doll's house, in front of an immaculate stretch of rolling lawn, George Carter's East Anglian home is what he terms 'a most satisfactory sort of house'. It would be hard to disagree. Its south façade, facing the gardens, is symmetrically arranged, with generous sash windows top and bottom at each side, and another immediately above the half-glazed front door. Here is plain rustic architecture at its best, pleasing in its simplicity, yet solid and dependable too. Sheltered from the local winds by a belt of trees to the west, and orientated to capture the best of the day's sun, it has been planned with canny economy.

So it's a surprise to hear local rumour that the house was designed on the back of a cigarette packet by the local landowner. Even more so, to learn that it was built in the 1920s to resemble a plain eighteenth-century farmhouse. The property was built as the home farm for the local estate. The cluster of adjoining farm buildings to the north side are much earlier, dated 1835.

George Carter, already living in East Anglia, liked the house from the moment he saw it. 'It sits in the middle of its land – and it's a house that engages with its garden,' he says. As he is a garden designer himself, with commissions on both sides of the Atlantic, this was an appealing quality. Most farmhouses, he adds, sit to one side of their accompanying land.

His home also enjoys a pleasingly remote setting. Interested visitors to George's garden (arranged by appointment only) will find themselves driving down criss-crossing narrow lanes with barely another property in sight. And when they do arrive, after passing mature woods to the north, there are uninterrupted views from the house for a good eight miles. George doesn't mind the silence or lack of neighbours. During the day the house, which incorporates his office on the north side, and the adjoining outbuildings are the focus for his garden design business. By night, he has the garden to himself.

With its central position, the house effectively bisects its hectare (two-plus acres) of land, forming a division between the working buildings and the formal domestic gardens to the south. Since George moved here in 1990, the principal entrance has become the garden door. Pass inside, and the compact floor plan is evident. From the central hall, you can turn right into the drawing room and left into the dining room. Behind the hall is the old scullery (now the utility room) and, beyond that, George's office (reached by a separate front door). Behind the dining room is the kitchen. He explains that the drawing room, which nowadays spans the full depth of the house, had already been knocked through when he took possession. The back half of this room was once the farm's dairy.

Some houses are so perfect in their simplicity that there's no need (not to mention physical scope) to change the floor plan, and this was the case for George. The size also suited him: no matter, he says, that the dining room is just 3.5 m (12 ft) square, because it is easy to heat, and always warm. 'I never wanted a cavernous country house!' he adds. Yet the ceilings in the rooms are generously high, at over 2.5 m (almost 9 ft). He is not surprised at the small proportions, pointing out that such abstemiousness with materials was the result of post-war building policies. 'If a property was built under a certain floor area, builders were eligible for grants,' he says. Its post-war status no doubt also accounts for its

simple construction. The house is built from oddly shaped East Anglian red bricks, recycled at a time when resources were low.

Despite its small rooms, there is a gentle elegance to George's modest farmhouse. The colour palette is restrained, veering from off-whites downstairs to palest grey in his bedroom and a grey-green drab in the dining room. Despite the description, this looks pretty by day, even better by night when it sets off the decorative gilding. It is also an unmatchable colour: George created it by mixing leftover paint samples. All the woodwork for the outbuildings, from the French doors into the orangery to the gates leading from one farmyard to the next, are also painted in varying shades of gardener's green. The knocked-back colours are deliberate. 'The pale colours go with English weather,' says George. They also direct attention back outside, to the gardens, which are monochromatic. Because the windows are symmetrically placed, he adds, it is easy to arrange pleasing views from any room, and the garden's vistas align with the windows and doors.

Each room is plain and serviceable, which is perhaps part of the appeal. Architecturally, the ceilings and walls are adorned with nothing fancier than a waist-high dado rail. In the hall and kitchen, George retained what are probably the original terracotta tiles, but over the concrete floors elsewhere (laid decades before) he has put coir matting, and there are 'the cheapest possible' calico

the dining room, the plain reeded Regency-style surround was made up to his design.

When George first arrived, the fireplace in the drawing room needed to be opened up, and wasn't symmetrical. He installed a plain surround, then panelled the entire wall, so as to cheat the eye into a sense of symmetry. He also inserted two antique doors either side of the fireplace, behind which he stores a collection of antique china and glass.

What the room lacks in area, he has made up for by cleverly picking furniture that works with, rather than against, the modest proportions. He designed the sofa (upholstered in striped mattress ticking) extra low so as not to impede the view across the room, and beneath the north-facing window sits a lean, elegant 1820s chaise longue. Paintings and mirrors are also small-scale, so as not to be overpowering, although he has included a few large sculptures and urns to add contrasting scale.

It is outside, perhaps, where George has created the biggest transformation, reflecting the symmetrical theme of the house in the gardens and grounds. In the early stages, when he first moved in, he concentrated on building the two bricks walls that flank the south façade, and the box hedging. 'By doing this I was able to key the house into the landscape,' he comments.

curtains hanging at the windows. The biggest project was to reinstate sympathetic-looking chimneypieces in place of the unattractive 1960s ones that were in place when he moved in. In the upstairs study-bedroom, George reused a bolection-moulded fire surround that he had designed for an exhibition. In

ABOVE *The house's design means that every room captures the best of the rural and garden views. In front of the window stands a green-painted early nineteenth-century chair, with a rush seat.*

Immediately in front of the south façade is a formal parterre, featuring silvery grey dwarf curry plants (*Helichrysum angustifolium*) framed with clipped box. Beyond that, separated by more box hedging, there is what was once a tennis lawn, now used for croquet, and then open fields. Stand in the centre of the lawn, and to either side there are twin open lattice pavilions, painted in soothing grey-green. At the far end of the lawn stands a rusticated obelisk.

Yet for every ordered garden vista, there is a surprise one, too. Visitors to George's office, coming out of the north door, need only to turn right to see one of his trademark 'tool' gates, quirkily featuring criss-crossed garden forks, spades and hoes. Far beyond that, flanked by clipped box 2.5 m (8 ft) tall, you can glimpse a flint obelisk. Wander around the grounds and you will come across, in turn, the orchard, the pond, the herb garden and the enticingly named 'wiggly walk', which links the far end of the croquet lawn to the orchard. Within the linked three farmyards, enclosed on three sides by assorted barns

LEFT *Throughout the formal gardens, box hedging has been used to create vistas and avenues. Here, a reconstituted stone urn, sitting on a flint plinth, is set into a niche cut into the hedge. The low trellis encasing the beds of lavender and box was made to George Carter's own design, though based on a seventeenth-century style.*
ABOVE *In the orangery, once a cow byre, George over winters tender plants. Here an auricula theatre is half-obscured behind a bench made to George's own design.*

and open cart-sheds, are more surprises: a wall fountain, obelisks and a green sentry box.

It is in the double-height barn that much of the day-time life of George's farm exists, as it acts as an outdoor room particularly good for large parties. In the central section of what was a cow shed, there are grey-painted French doors leading into the orangery. Here, in winter, shelter George's giant orange and lemon trees, and in summer, it is filled with assorted columns, urns and benches waiting to be incorporated into a garden design (he also designs gardens and exhibits at prestigious shows such as the Chelsea Flower Show). As for the open cart-sheds, they provide more storage, as fresh pieces arrive or new designs are worked on. 'In summer, I also use one of them as an al fresco dining room,' adds George. Proving that the best English houses – and their outbuildings – are flexible and sociable too.

LEFT & ABOVE

In the simple, elegant drawing room, decorative accessories are in keeping with the modest panelling and low ceilings. Above the fire surround hangs an eighteenth-century glass picture and, below it, a slightly later French mirror with its original mercury silvering. The European walnut chest of drawers dates from the late seventeenth century, and is flanked by a pair of chairs bearing their original paint. George has been collecting antiques for many years, and the portrait hanging above the chest of drawers was his first-ever purchase, an oil painting bought for £3. A panelled cupboard holds a collection of late eighteenth-century Newhall china, a Staffordshire factory.

ABOVE & RIGHT

The long, low drawing room, which runs the full depth of the house, is divided up into different seating areas, and has several occasional tables for books and decorative objects. Against one wall sits the contrasting arrangement of a 1940s plaster sculpture of a woman and a mahogany Pembroke table. The elegant 1820s chaise in the drawing room is flanked by an unusual assortment of pieces: to the left, there is a modern glass uplighter, and to the right, an 1800 mahogany chair, with a plain Scottish mirror hanging just above it.

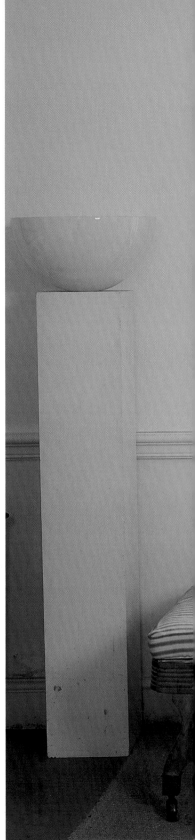

OPPOSITE & ABOVE

Among George's collection of antique furniture, he mixes in his own designs, some originally created for garden

designs or exhibitions. In the hall, one wall is dominated by his Italian Baroque-style console table, over hung with a

mirror designed for the Chelsea Flower Show. In the diminutive dining room, the fireplace is dominated by a letter-

cutting exercise, found by George at an art school, and probably post-war. On the same wall hangs a Regency convex

mirror, with the customary eagle above.

LEFT & ABOVE

One of the bedrooms has been transformed into a reading room, with the addition of floor-to-ceiling bookshelves and a battered leather Edwardian consulting couch. The leopard skin throw, tossed across it, belonged to George's aunt. On the light and sunny landing, there is an intriguing collection of objects, including a wall-mounted cast for an urn, designed by George, and a 1950s brass chandelier.

OPPOSITE

One corner of the master bedroom is dominated by a plaster bust depicting Thucydides, the first Greek historian. It is a copy of the original marble bust, from Holkham Hall, available from the Holkham collection.

OPPOSITE & ABOVE

The formal landscaped gardens are characterized throughout by George's structural designs. The trellised gazebo is one of a pair, each holding a bust of Ceres, and built with a bench from which to enjoy the morning and evening views to the east and west. The garden gate is an example of George's tool gate designs. Elsewhere, a pair of flint obelisks, 3 m (10 ft) high, stand by the orchard.

RIGHT

In the northern part of the garden, backed by oaks and beeches, there is a large, peaceful pond. To protect local duck life from marauding foxes, it has been fitted with a floating duck island and a secure nesting box.

East Anglia

GOTHICK FOLLY

It seems a peculiarly English habit to find the house of a lifetime by chance, often after an exhaustive, and increasingly fruitless, search. So it was for John Stevenson and Charles Moss. They spotted details of their eighteenth-century Gothick folly in a back-street Ipswich estate agent. Intrigued, they asked for details, only to have the estate agent initially refuse to show it, because it was in such a disgraceful state of disrepair. At the time the folly was inhabited by a tramp (albeit a well-educated one with a penchant for good architecture), and the surrounding parkland was overgrown. 'But of course by that stage we were hooked,' says John.

Thus began a thirty-year love affair with this romantic building. The folly sits squarely in 1.5 ha (4 acres) of grounds, surrounded in turn by 8 ha (20 acres) of flat East Anglian parkland. With its soaring arched windows and fairytale castellated parapet, it's easy to spot late eighteenth-century Gothick revival influences. It has been dated by the architect Sir Hugh Casson, John says, at between 1790 and 1810. Its decorative exterior gives more than a nod to that most exuberant of high-Gothick castellated villas of the era, Horace Walpole's Strawberry Hill, just west of London. Yet its comparatively modest size and symmetrical design make for a welcoming home. Built from brick and distinctive local flint, it has successfully weathered over two hundred years of raw East Anglian winds.

As to its origins, John repeats the charming local legend that the house was built by the local landowner's land agent. In the late eighteenth century, the surrounding area was thickly wooded, and he is reputed to have built himself a 'secret' house - without the earl's permission - concealed among the trees. On the north façade of the folly there are two lancet windows, measuring 1.2 m (4 ft) high by an unusually generous 60 cm (2 ft) wide: just enough space for the errant land agent to escape, should the landowner make an unexpected appearance!

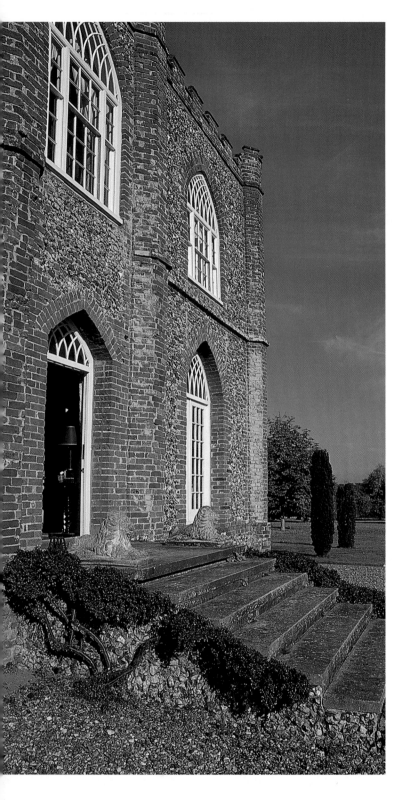

Over the generations, the folly has taken on a number of names, from Page's Folly (when one Captain Page lived there) to King's Folly. But by the time John and Charles finally arrived on the scene, it had been unceremoniously divided up into two separate dwellings and needed a lot of loving care.

Today, it has been painstakingly restored, as have the surrounding gardens. The land immediately in front of the house is mown grass and there's a gravel drive (it's a house rule that cars, however, park at the back), but formal gardens extend in front of the south façade, beyond the pond. Guests to the folly can wander among the curved herbaceous borders or enjoy over a hundred roses in the rose garden, then stray as far as the orchard of mixed fruit trees. The gardens, John says, were designed from scratch. One of the earliest projects was to restore a brick and flint perimeter wall to contain the formal planting. A shepherd's cottage a few minutes' walk from the house, has also been renovated, and serves as a guest cottage. It's linked to the main house by a semi-circle of limes, planted by John and Charles to replace mature elm trees lost in the great storm of 1987.

It's a given that no one buys a Gothick-inspired building without an inherent love of the style's

LEFT & OPPOSITE *Today, the striking Gothick fenestration has been restored, but when the owners took on the house, the original brick arches had been scrappily filled in with conventional square windows. The flint turret at the north west corner (opposite) is purely decorative.*

soaring and dramatic features. Even at first glance, John and Charles were able to see beyond the existing small, square windows to the outline of the original Gothick frames, 2.7 m (9 ft) high and ringed with brick, that, when reinstated, would dominate the south façade. For them, this was a chief attraction, and the rubble that had filled them in, probably for generations, was cleared away in the early stages of renovation, and new fenestration added. Gradually, the house offered up more secrets. Intrigued that the squat doors inside the house seemed so out of keeping with the high ceilings, John gingerly took his hammer to the plaster and revealed the original arched double doorways leading into the principal rooms.

Such early investigations were just the start. There were a total of seven staircases criss-crossing the divided property, oddly sprouting from a breakfast room and a dining room. These were gradually removed as John and Charles strove to return the building to its original floor layout. 'We never had a grand master plan, and we are still working on the house,' comments John. Now there are a conventional two staircases: one leading upstairs from the hall, and the other to the basement, which houses a wine cellar and utility area. In the cellar, says John, they found the remains of an Elizabethan brick oven. And the pond was 'discovered', grassed over, after they realized that the grass looked particularly verdant at the front of the house.

Walk up the short flight of stone steps today, with

the peaceful pond to your back, and mature oaks, elms, chestnuts and limes dotted across the parkland, and you're in for a vivid surprise. Tongue-in-cheek, John describes the interior of the house now as a 'gaudy gypsy caravan' of a place, crammed with several decades' worth of acquisitions, as well as a sensory explosion of colour. In fact, the striking shades - starting with sulphur yellow in the hall and a soft salmon in the drawing room - are well-orchestrated tributes to the collector and builder William Beckford (1760-1844). John researched Beckford's own folly, Fonthill Abbey in Wiltshire, and loosely based his choices on the extravagant original colours there.

John has done much of the decoration himself. The

drawing room walls were meticulously painted with four coats of white eggshell, followed by six coats of pink. He adds that the colour, which has mellowed over the years into a gloriously antique finish, was inspired by the dust jacket for Sir Kenneth Clark's book, *Gothick Revival*. In the dining room, the walls are a dense alizarin crimson (a technical shade of artist's gouache, taken from a paintbox), teamed with a flamboyant antique Turkish carpet on the floor, and 170 m (185 yd) of midnight blue cambric tenting the ceiling. Upstairs, one of the bedrooms is painted in evocative Cooking Apple Green (one of the historic colours from the Farrow & Ball range), contrasted with raspberry silk hangings (also made by John) on the four-poster bed.

Look at the richly decorated rooms, with their Gothick-moulded cornice work and matching pelmets, and it's tempting to assume that these features, too, have been carefully restored. In truth, no internal

details remained. Undaunted, John opened his address book and called up scenic artist George Galitzine, who at the time was designing lavish sets for Pink Floyd. Together he and John designed and executed new fibreglass mouldings. Panelled, Gothick double doors were made to order by a local joiner, then painted in grey drab, with off-white and gilded detailing on the mouldings. It was impossible to salvage the original timber floors, which had long rotted away. Instead, faux marble linoleum was laid in the hall, and star-emblazoned linoleum in the dining room.

With an eye ever on Gothick influences, over the years John and Charles have inherited and amassed a quirky collection of appropriate furniture, without turning each room into a pastiche. In the formal dining room, an enviable set of painted Gothick-inspired chairs surround the table: John reveals that there is just one 1750 original (found in a local antique shop) and the rest of the set were made to match. In the blue-painted bedroom, the 1920s headboard is attributed to Ambrose Heal, of Heal's. Then, of course, there is the latest acquisition, an 1812 longcase Gothick clock, standing in the sulphur yellow hall

ABOVE & OPPOSITE *One of the owners' earliest projects was to restore the brick and flint perimeter wall that now encloses the formal gardens. From here, an arch leads through into the orchard, and an original early nineteenth-century timber door opens into the lesser walled garden. Around the archway is trained 'Zéphirine Drouhin', a magnificent rose with no thorns.*

where it marks time with an appealing chime.

Clusters of colourful knick-knacks cover every surface. Charles's collection of turquoise opaline glass is set against the salmon pink of the drawing room, in an outrageous clash of which Beckford himself might have been proud.

It's appealing to hear that, in John's and Charles's opinion, even after thirty years they are still adding, and subtracting, in search of their perfect rendition of the Gothick-inspired home. 'We will always approach it in a light-hearted vein,' John is quick to point out. Now plans are afoot to change the grand Gothick windows downstairs. When the glass was originally fitted, they had decided to have French windows for each of the ground-floor rooms, forgetting - in their eagerness - the 1 m (3 ft) drop to ground level. 'We've cursed our decision ever since!' John adds. For a while, they toyed with the idea of adding a short flight of steps, for descending gracefully into the garden. Now, they have resolved to replace the French doors with sashes to match the first-floor windows.

It is, they conclude, these same windows that make the house the joyful and welcoming home it has always been. 'There are wonderful views from every room, and the house is always filled with beautiful light,' comments John. It's hard not to feel sorry for that errant land agent, who - surrounded by secret woodland - may never have enjoyed those lovely long vistas across the broad East Anglian countryside.

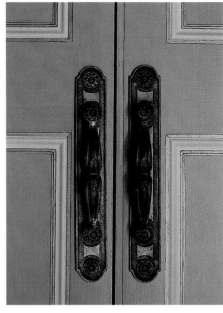

LEFT & ABOVE

In the striking yellow hall, an intriguing mix of antique furniture and Gothick pieces set a light-hearted tone in keeping with the style of the building. Eighteenth-century candle sconces flank a pretty antique mirror, and on the marble-topped Louis XV-style console sits a key-cupboard disguised as a miniature Gothick house. The 1812 Gothick longcase clock is a recent addition. Early twentieth-century Spanish handles add a decorative flourish to new, Gothick-inspired doors, which lead into the drawing room.

OPPOSITE

The doorways to the principal rooms leading off the hall were concealed when the owners arrived, but are now highlighted with an ornate painted frieze.

LEFT & ABOVE

In the drawing room, with its soft salmon-coloured walls, John and Charles have amassed an eclectic collection of furniture and decorative pieces. The fireplace is flanked with two chiffoniers: the one to the left is early nineteenth-century English, with Gothick detailing, and the painted one to the right is eighteenth-century, decorated with gold figures. Above the fireplace is an oil painting, depicting pensioners at Greenwich discussing the Battle of the Nile. On the chiffonier sits Charles's collection of eyecatching Victorian opaline glass.

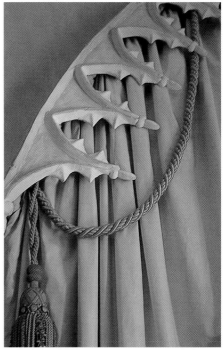

LEFT

Every corner of the drawing room is crammed with unusual pieces. An English green-painted table, topped with black marble, sits beneath an 1825 painted Gothick mirror, bought from a London antiques shop.

ABOVE & OPPOSITE

Much thought has gone into the decorative scheme for the room. The colour of the salmon-pink walls was inspired by the dust jacket for Sir Kenneth Clark's book, Gothick Revival, *and new fibreglass Gothick pelmets and plaster cornices were designed by scenic artist George Galitzine. It was he who moulded this elaborate ceiling rose on the drawing room ceiling.*

LEFT & ABOVE

In the dining room, the walls have been painted a dense crimson, with a tented ceiling in midnight blue cambric. The fine 1810 sideboard, made by Scottish cabinet-maker George Smith, is mahogany inlaid with ebony. On it sits a display of antique Spode meat platters, while above hangs a painting by Dawson-Watson, the English impressionist painter. The metal Venetian chandelier, with glass stem, also dates from 1810, and is one of a pair. Sitting on a pretty 1920s painted chest of drawers is a collection of eighteenth- and nineteenth-century decanters and water jugs.

LEFT & OPPOSITE

The Gothick theme is repeated upstairs. In the guest bedroom, the Ambrose Heal bedhead from the 1920s, is echoed in an arched Gothick chair. The walls are painted in Farrow & Ball's Dix Blue, and the curtain fabric is a Sanderson archive print. The bed is covered with an antique embroidered wool coverlet. Hanging above the faux painted silver birch chest of drawers is a very pretty eighteenth-century carved wooden mirror. The china King Charles spaniels are from a collection housed in the study.

LEFT & ABOVE

In the master bedroom, the George IV four-poster bed has been hung with raspberry silk, contrasted with cushions in Colefax & Fowler's Ribbon chintz. The walls are painted in Farrow & Ball's traditional Cooking Apple Green, and the Gothick-inspired frieze was designed by Johnand painted by specialist painter Billy Dix. On one wall hangs a fine eighteenth-century oil portrait (of an unknown gentleman), painted by the artist George Romney. To the right of door stands a capacious late eighteenth-century Scottish clothes press.

GOTHICK FOLLY

ABOVE & RIGHT

The pond at the front of the folly had been filled in years ago, but a tell-tale bright green on the lawns alerted the current owners to its location. It has now been restored and is planted with three weeping willows. The pond has become a haven not just for water hens and ducks, but carp and tench too.

VICTORIAN TERRACE HOUSE

In London, there's no escape from the never-ending Victorian terraces, row upon row of modest houses which then – and now – supplied ordinary domestic dwellings to the working city population. Whether skirting city squares, lining quiet streets or sitting companionably cheek by jowl with modern architecture, their familiar façades are as much a part of London as any of the major historical buildings. According to the district or street, they may be stucco-fronted or in brick, grand or small, but apart from minor details, there's little variation from one terrace to the next.

Yet perhaps it is this very similarity that makes these Victorian homes so intriguing. How, wonders the casual passer-by, does one particular house differ from its next-door neighbour? Will it feel the same, boast the same features? And precisely because of their narrow, buttoned-up faces, there's an even greater temptation to explore, to find out who lives here and what lies inside. In rural houses, there's usually a long drive or at least a carefully tended front garden to prepare the visitor for the characteristics they'll find within. But in the city terrace, with just a short flight of anonymous steps between approach and arrival, the surprise is immediate. Such is the case with the intriguing London home of Ann Mollo and Jon Bunker. Step over the threshold and you're transported into an unusual and all-enveloping interior.

The house is tucked towards one end of a typical city terrace, close to a pretty square near west London's Holland Park. It was built in 1850, at the same time as the square. It's a solid-looking, three-storey house with a basement, but nevertheless a modest early Victorian house, built even in those days to cater for a relatively lowly cross-section of people – houses for the grander middle classes were built around the square itself. Ann bought it in the 1960s it for a tantalizing £8000. 'I didn't pick it on architectural merit; in fact, these houses are very badly built,' she says. 'It was derelict and cheap – just what I needed at the time.'

She has lived here for forty years. If that's unusual for London, given the capital's transient population, it's still more surprising to hear how little she has changed the property over time. In a city obsessed with gutting properties, 'doing them up', then moving on, it's refreshing to hear that the sitting room walls are still painted the same shade Ann had commissioned in the 1960s. Some renovation work was immediate: only one original fireplace remained, and all the cornices and dado rails were long gone. But otherwise, here is a house that has gradually evolved over the years, reflecting in little that gradual process of accumulation that takes place in period country houses up and down the country.

Given Ann's profession, and that of her partner Jon, it is no surprise that the house is decorative and densely filled. She is an acclaimed film set designer, and has worked on prestigious projects such as *Greystoke* and *The French Lieutenant's Woman*. Jon is a film production designer. Both have a passion for collecting, and a shared love of all things Gothick. Over the years, Ann has fed her habit for collecting while trawling antique shops and markets in search of film props, and has only stopped now because, quite simply, the house is full. 'I buy what I like,' she says.

Wander from one packed room to the next, and 'what I like' covers myriad categories: there are collections and pictures of lions and houses, birds, dogs and horses, and shelves groaning with plain eighteenth-century Staffordshire creamware, a particular favourite. On the first floor, between the drawing room and the library, there is even a small room dubbed the Creamware Room, where much of it is on display. If it's a peculiarly English habit to collect avidly, it is all the more appealing to hear that Ann's impetus isn't investment - 'nothing I have is of any particular value' - but simply a love of intriguing objects. Everything here is carefully collated and mounted, from a series of dog pictures in the yellow television room, to massed Victorian rice-paper paintings in the bedroom.

A visitor to the Victorian terrace may come to expect typically small rooms leading off to the right- or left-hand side of a narrow hall, according to where the staircase lies. Yet, as you wander around Ann Mollo's house, there's an Alice-in-Wonderland sense that all is not what it seems, and that there's a higher than normal room count on each floor. The reason for this is that the house is linked to its neighbour. Ann's mother had lived next door, and after she died Ann and Jon joined the two houses together at every level except on the ground floor, effectively doubling the living quarters. For once,

OPPOSITE *English light is a recurrent theme. Sunshine floods the landing from a double height stairwell and there is a view of the Gothick-style garden, with a late Georgian stone urn (one of three acquired for a film set) in pride of place. Every surface in the house displays treasures. This narrow ledge holds Victorian jugs, a Wedgwood pearlware jardiniere and an eighteenth-century carved wooden candlestick.*

the unwavering internal plan for the standard Victorian terrace - front room, back room, scullery and kitchen, downstairs, with the bedrooms upstairs - has been well and truly foxed.

Now, on entering the front door of the right-hand house (Ann's original house) you can turn to the left, into the dining room and Ann's study, or ascend the stairs to a first-floor drawing room. From the drawing room, you pass through the Creamware Room (originally a first-floor bedroom) into the adjacent house. On this floor Ann and Jon have created a Gothick-inspired library. Go upstairs again and, directly above it is the television room. Linking this room to the original bedroom in the right-hand house, there is a long narrow Gothick-styled walk-through bathroom, with a dressing room composed of wall-to-wall mirrored wardrobes.

This is a colourful house, a far cry from the taupe and white that characterizes the palette of

'restored' London houses. The vivid yellow in the television room was picked 'because it's a good Georgian yellow', and the grey-blue of the Gothick library cupboards was perfectly matched to the shade of a favourite photo album. The bedroom, Ann says, has always been green, in one varying shade or another. In the drawing room the walls have been painted by Cyril Whapshot (he was a specialist painter for John Fowler) in two shades of palest melon. Its delicate tones have withstood the test of time. They look as good today with the three matching antique Aubusson pelmets that now frame the windows as they did in the 1960s with a quite different set of curtains.

A visitor to the house can't fail to notice the decorative Gothick theme throughout, which is a light-hearted tribute to the fanciful Strawberry Hill style. Jon designed the bespoke cabinets in the bathroom and dressing room, as well as the wall-to-wall glass-fronted library cupboards, stuffed to the gills with books on antiques and design. The door to the television room is also Gothick: it was bought at an antique fair, then the doorway remoulded to fit. With self-mocking grandeur, even the TV resides in a Gothick-style cupboard, which Jon bought as an old font cover, and reworked as a cabinet. 'Gothick

ABOVE *The walls of the stairwell are hung with a themed collection of watercolours, each depicting an English house. Behind the drawing room door hangs an eighteenth-century French Rococo wallpaper panel: to the right is an English chiffonier.*

ABOVE *The bathroom is decorated with a fretted Gothick-cum-Shaker-inspired frieze by Jon, and from it hangs a Victorian Gothick lamp.*

detailing simply appeals to us, and - as a style - it's inherently English,' says Ann.

Her other passion is for Regency chinoiserie furniture, and it is evident throughout the house, most particularly in the bedroom. In here, there is a pretty Regency bamboo chest of drawers, flanked by simulated bamboo chairs from the same period. Above it hangs a framed decorative panel, which may have originated in a chinoiserie-panelled room. And the pair of large mirrors, behind the bed and on the adjacent wall, was designed by Jon to match the room, and then cast in plastic fibreglass. 'He also designed the faux bamboo cornice,' Ann adds. Keen as they were on comparatively modest cornices, the Victorians would most likely have approved.

No doubt they would have approved, too, of the well-filled rooms at Ann Mollo's home, given the Victorian penchant for cluttered interiors, fabric hangings and decorative treasures in every spare corner. Returning down the stairs and back into the original house, you pass from the hall into Ann's study, which is the most densely filled room of all: it is from here that she now pursues her new career of garden design. To the rear of the house is the mature garden she has evolved over the years: it is filled with English roses, clematis and perennials, with a series of Gothick arches dividing up the greenery.

Between Ann's study, which overlooks the street, and the kitchen to the rear, is a tiny dining room, separated from her office by a pair of arched glass double doors, dated around 1860. They were originally inner doors to a London club, and Ann bought them after she had hired them for a film set. It is perhaps the confident mix of furniture in the dining room that explains why this house is such an appealing sum of its many parts. The table, in stainless steel and black glass, was designed in 1980 by George Ciancimino. It has been teamed with a set of Regency chairs. Clearly Ann really does buy what she likes, with one eye on the past and the other just as firmly on the future.

LEFT & ABOVE

In the Georgian yellow TV room, the Gothick theme is played out with a television
cabinet, adapted from a font cover, and a Gothick door bought from an antique fair.
A decorative wooden fire surround, designed by the owner, replaces the original
mantelpiece. Arranged above it are Victorian rice paper flower pictures, and on it, there's
a pair of eighteenth-century creamware mugs, and four French faience *plates. On the*
other side of the room, clustered above an early nineteenth-century sofa, is a collection
of watercolours of dogs. The black American Hitchcock chair, one of a pair, is from the
mid nineteenth century.

ABOVE & OPPOSITE

In the upstairs library glazed Gothick style cabinets, designed by Ann and Jon, hold
their vast collection of design and antiques books. There's room here to sit and read
at the mahogany Georgian tea table, on two early nineteenth-century painted chairs.
The Gothick theme continues in the drawing room, with a pair of black painted
chiffoniers standing either side of the fireplace. The elaborate steel fireguard was once
part of an altar, and Ann bought the Victorian horse painting above the fireplace many
years ago, for £100. Antique Aubusson panels frame the windows.

LEFT & ABOVE

Tucked between Ann's study and the kitchen is the dining area. Teaming the contemporary stainless steel and black glass table, by George Ciancimino, with a set of English Regency chairs is typical of Ann's eclectic taste. Flanking the gilded mirror above the table is a pair of seventeenth-century church wall sconces from Italy. Ann's extensive collection of eighteenth- and early nineteenth-century English creamware is displayed throughout the house. The dining table is set with a selection, more is arranged on the kitchen dresser, but the vast majority are upstairs in the Creamware Room, where a huge range of different pieces are carefully arranged on blue-painted open shelves.

LEFT & ABOVE

In the green-painted master bedroom there is a Regency-inspired Chinoiserie theme. The surround to the large mirror above the bed and the faux bamboo cornice were designed by Jon, and cast in fibreglass. Above the Regency chest of drawers hangs a nineteenth-century panel, bought from Guinevere Antiques, which may have originally been part of the panelling in a Chinese room. On the walls are hung a collection of Victorian rice paper flower paintings. Softening the Regency simulated bamboo sofa is a mix of new and antique textile cushions.

When Ann and Jon joined the two town houses together, the bathroom was redone. A newly formed Gothick doorway now provides a link between the properties. The mirror, vanity unit and bath surround was all designed by Jon, with Gothick arches, while the painted armoire is an old piece, repainted to match its surroundings. A modern flat weave rug by David Black covers the floor.

OPPOSITE

Adjacent to the master bathroom, Ann Mollo has a formal dressing room. On each wall stands a pair of painted and mirrored Gothick-style cupboards, designed by Jon, and in the centre sits a shell-design painted Victorian hall chair. A very pretty Regency dressing mirror, set with candles, stands decoratively to one side.

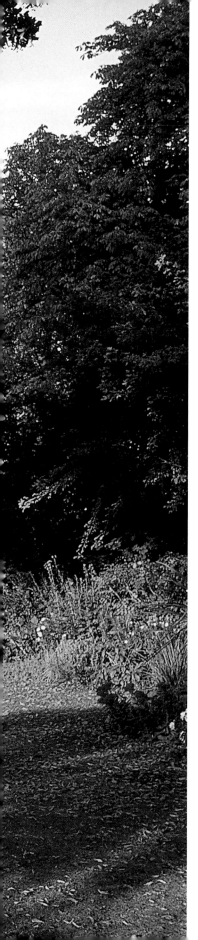

GEORGIAN COUNTRY HOUSE

'English houses evolve so beautifully,' says Inge Sprawson. 'They're also more comfortable than those on the continent.' Austrian by birth, but long ago settled in England, she's more than qualified to comment. As the owner of a Grade II* listed house, near Glastonbury, Somerset, she has also had first-hand experience. After all, her country home – set among 2 ha (5 acres) of walled gardens and cider apple orchards – has been graciously evolving for over 350 years. It began life as a modest Jacobean farmhouse (circa 1645), and over the next two centuries it was elegantly extended. In 1760 a pretty south-facing Georgian façade was added, then in 1820 came a Regency wing. In the early twenty-first century, she and her husband Robert are still restoring the estate, and it has once again become a comfortable family home.

Inge is never surprised when visitors exclaim: 'This is my favourite house!' She, too, felt a welcoming vibe when she tracked down the property twelve years ago. It was in a desperate state of repair, with water pouring through the roof, and furnishings literally in tatters. Yet it offered just the architectural style she was set on: high ceilings and elegant proportions, one step up from a traditional farmhouse. It is, she sums up, 'a small big house'. In other words, it has the elaborate detailing of a country manor house, but on an acceptable domestic scale. As Inge, an haute couture dress designer, and her lawyer husband both divide their time between London and the West Country, they didn't want a vast country pile.

If it was daunting to undertake such a project (the restoration is still going on), the Sprawsons have no regrets. They found an excellent builder and made the necessary repairs, but had no intention of altering its internal structure. 'We didn't want to change a thing.' Now, they have made the house their own. It exudes an air of restrained elegance and comfort, and is filled with a mix of family heirlooms, some from their London base, and a few newly purchased from local antiques shops. Like all the best English houses, it is a sociable, welcoming property. It easily accommodates extra guests (the Sprawsons' son, Rupert, and his family often visit at weekends), yet it's companionable, rather than echoing and empty, when there are just the two of them, not forgetting Hector the weimaraner and Horace the dachshund.

Although the Sprawsons still use the original front door in the Jacobean wing, guests usually arrive at the south-facing garden door. As you enter, a sense of timelessness descends. There's the evergreen scent of waxed floorboards and garden flowers, and from outside the drawing room you can hear the fountain in the Italianate garden beyond. Pass into what the family now call the library hall, and to the right there is the dining room, and to the left the formal drawing room. Straight on, the original staircase leads up to the first floor. Yet visitors often find themselves lingering in the hall. It is cosily furnished with books, a sofa and the original open fire, and doubles as a casual sitting room.

Ask about the pitch pine which lines an imposing archway or, for that matter, any of the wooden doors, staircase panelling and arch surrounds, and the history of the house unfurls. Nothing is known of the original Jacobean inhabitants, but in the mid eighteenth century it passed to a new owner. Inge tells the enticing tale of an urchin boy, wandering on the nearby moors, who went to Bristol to seek his fortune, and became first a tobacconist, then a successful shipping merchant. That boy was Mr Field, and it was

he who added the Georgian wing to the house. 'The pitch pine panelling in the house was brought home from America, originally used as ballast on the ships,' says Inge. Mr Field married Miss Ruscombe, and in 1820 their daughter, Miss Ruscombe Field, added the Regency wing.

The house, of course, has finally passed to the Sprawsons. During the twentieth century, family tragedies and lack of funds had resulted in its demise, though there is a happy ending: the daughter of the late last owner now lives close by, in a converted coach house in the grounds. Given that an ancient property is the sum, not just of its architectural parts, but of the lives played out in it, this suits Inge. 'The house has the feeling of old gentry about it,' she says. 'The inhabitants have loved it and got married in it and died in it – somehow you can feel that in the walls.' There's a strong spirit of history in the garden, too. Inge points to the three giant lime trees outside the drawing room, which she fondly refers to as the 'three sisters'. 'They were planted to celebrate the Battle of Waterloo.'

It was for all these reasons that Inge and Robert have restored with restraint, wanting to keep as close

OPPOSITE *Access to the house from the nearby lane is via a new wooden gate set between period stone pineapple-topped pillars. The pedimented door is characteristically Georgian, but the intricate iron balustrade is thought to be Victorian, probably a replacement for its earlier Georgian counterpart.*

ABOVE *Surrounded by three ancient lime trees, just opposite the south façade of the house, is a stone gazebo, probably built at the same time as the house's Regency wing. Today, its ground floor provides a decorative housing for the modern swimming pool pump, and on the upper floor, which has a coved ceiling, there is a desk and a fireplace.*

as possible to the original mood of the house. Upstairs, there was certainly much work to be done: the roof had to be repaired, and four new bathrooms were added, discreetly fitted into old linen cupboards, so that the changes did not to disturb the layout of the first floor. On the top floor, the two attic rooms, almost certainly the original servants' quarters, have been converted into guest bedrooms and a bathroom. Now, the principal bedrooms and bathrooms are decorated in a palette of soft, watery English colours, the curtains and four-poster beds hung with linens and cottons in historical designs. One of the bedrooms retains its original Georgian panelling, and all the marble fireplaces, window shutters and wide oak floorboards remain.

It is downstairs that Inge has kept particularly close to what attracted her to the house in the first place. The hall is painted in the same muted salmon shade that has survived for years. And in the light and elegant drawing room, the walls are untouched, left just as they were eighty years ago. 'It's that wonderful apple colour you sometimes see in English houses – not dull, quite bright – a very special colour,' says Inge enthusiastically. When the house was sold, the owner also left a pair of sofas, which came originally from her family home not far away in Dunster Castle. The covers were almost in shreds, but Inge has had the sofas upholstered in a similar fabric by Colefax & Fowler. In the dining room, the decoration has also required a little helping hand. The damask print wallpaper was beyond repair, but Inge was keen to retain it, so she asked Zoffany to copy it, and faithfully recovered the walls.

Often it is the surviving architectural detailing that truly marks the character of a house. And it is the very fact that so much here is original that inspires Inge. The timber doors retain their eighteenth-century polished brass door furniture, every window has its shutters, and many shelves and cupboards are intact, proving that built-in furniture isn't just a contemporary feature. Prettiest of all, perhaps, are the timber-panelled shelves framed with a scalloped pelmet - one in the dining room, the other in the library hall. At floor level each of these has a cubby-hole, reputed to have been a resting place for the owners' lap-dogs. Also off the library hall (150 years ago, it was the dining room) is the butler's pantry, with its rows of shelves for glass and silver, and original cutlery drawers.

If there is anything that Inge has changed in this wonderful, enduring home, it has been a little gentle altering of room function, to suit Inge and Robert's modern-day needs. With its good proportions and three low-silled, wide Georgian windows (two overlooking the gardens to the south, one to the west) Inge decided that the large dining room would be better suited to what is now the elegant drawing room. Her dining room, consequently, is in the old drawing room: a generous room, nevertheless, as it seats up to twenty comfortably. In the basement, where the kitchens would have been a hundred years ago, she and Robert now have a utility area and a wine cellar. Her current kitchen is in the Jacobean wing, in what is thought to have once been the estate office. She is planning to move the kitchen into the old nursery, overlooking the orchard, but this requires special planning consent.

And that, perhaps, is the point of living in an old English house. It's satisfying to enjoy what has evolved before, but to add something of the current century, too. It's interesting to uncover what history you can, but to relish the secrets such a home holds as well. Inge remarks that there are several mysteries that will probably never be uncovered. One is the eagle perched atop the slate tiles on the Georgian wing. The name of the building's architect isn't known, but it's said that the eagle was his trademark, and there is at least one other Somerset house that bears it, too. The other curiosity is upstairs, on the first-floor landing. The distinctively curved wall, Inge says, is thought to be much older than the house, possibly part of an earlier tower. It's tempting to stand just for a moment, with your hand on the wall, and imagine how many human voices it has absorbed.

OPPOSITE, ABOVE & RIGHT

With its needlepoint rug, period oil paintings of sporting scenes, and mellow salmon-coloured walls, what is now called the library hall provides a welcome for visitors. From here, there is a direct view into the dining room. The main arch is lined with pitch pine, as is a smaller arch on the stairway, leading up to the bedrooms. On the staircase leading to the panelled guest bedroom the walls are clustered with a mix of contemporary family portraits, and an oil painting of the house, executed by a visiting Russian artist.

LEFT & ABOVE

The soft apple green walls of the drawing room haven't been repainted for eighty years. Some of the furniture here was passed on by the previous owner, including the Chinese lacquered cabinet, the convex mirror above the fireplace, with its extravagant dragon, and the raspberry pink sofas, though these have since been reupholstered. Flanking the Chinese cabinet is a pair of George II heavy mahogany chairs, bought by Inge at auction. In one corner stands a French inlaid commode with a marble top. The antique French chandelier, with its silk cord sheath, hangs from the original Regency ceiling rose, featuring an elaborate classical design of acanthus leaves.

The dining room is situated in the original Georgian part of the house, and looks
to the south, across the lawns. As the existing wallpaper was past being restored,
a fragment was copied by Zoffany, and now the walls have been repapered in the wine
red damask design. Above the fireplace hangs a contemporary maritime scene,
painted by a friend in the Dutch Old Master style. To the right, in an oval gilt frame,
is one of a pair of oil portraits of Inge's great-grandparents, and a pine-panelled
alcove holds a family collection of antique glasses.

LEFT & ABOVE

The master bedroom looks directly across the lawns to the south, with further views to the west. With its grey silk
curtains, and parchment-coloured walls, it is a light and sunny room, filled with a pretty collection of antiques.
Placed below one window, looking directly down on to the Italian garden, is an elegant Regency chaise longue,
and in the corner stands a late nineteenth-century French gilded screen. The fireplace is flanked by a diminutive pair
of Victorian nursery chairs, upholstered in silk damask, with a Venetian mirror above. In another corner, a painted
chair is drawn up to an antique Dutch bureau.

LEFT

In the guest bedroom directly above the dining room, the green-painted period panelling is complemented by a four-poster bed, made locally, to Inge's design. The bed and windows are draped with Beaumont and Fletcher linens. The dressing table lights on the Regency table at the window have shades depicting a watercolour after a Stubbs painting.

ABOVE

When the Sprawsons moved in, they had to add new bathrooms, often squeezing them into what were once dressing rooms or linen cupboards. At the entrance of the bathroom to the master bedroom stands a chest of drawers dating from 1800. The landscape above it was painted by a contemporary Russian artist.

ABOVE

Set among the extensive walled gardens are many unexpected garden statues, old and new – this horse's head, for example, is made from modern reconstituted stone, while the pineapple gate finial, is thought to date from the late eighteenth century. The pair to this, which had fallen into disrepair, was replaced early last century with a near-perfect copy.

RIGHT

The Italian garden, which the owners have carefully restored, is set immediately below the west-facing window in Inge's bedroom, so she can enjoy the gentle sound of the fountain. This spot, surrounded by a magnolia tree, clematis, and Italianate topiary, is a peaceful spot for al fresco meals.

Dorset

New Gothick House

Think of an English house, and it will be its age and history, just as much as any specific architectural style, which defines its character and appeal. Of course, every period has its fans: an owner may value a Jacobean farmhouse, an early Georgian manor or a Gothic school house, lovingly converted. But, over time, the charm of an old building is that it merges organically with the landscape, becoming a local landmark, sometimes a social focus, and it weathers gracefully with the prevailing climate. The gradual evolution of a house over the centuries is surely part of its intrinsic Englishness.

So there's no reason why - glimpsing imposing Bellamont House in the distance across the Dorset landscape - the first-time visitor shouldn't take at face value the eighteenth-century castellated country house they see standing before them. Set in the middle of 60 ha (150 acres) of its own land, and nestled into a coomb in the chalk downs that rise steeply just behind it, the house looks comfortably settled, as if it has stood here for centuries. Views from every window are of peacefully grazing cattle and sheep, uninterrupted except for the days when the sea mist rolls in across the land - Bellamont is just two miles from the south coast. This is home for Anthony and Harriet Sykes, an enviably tranquil spot, 'though it's quite windy, as we are 100 m [330 ft] above sea level, and we get the gentle south-west zephyrs,' says Anthony.

It's only when you draw up before the castellated entrance, with its family motto in high bronze lettering and family coats of arms upon the wall, that a question mark hovers. If you were to think, just momentarily, that the render looks marvellously pristine, or that the nail-studded doors are remarkably unravaged by two centuries of wind, then you would be right. The house is a mere seven years old and it was built in eight months. Beneath the subtle pink render sit plain concrete breeze blocks, not the ancient stone you might expect. Anthony remarks that, to the uninitiated visitor, there's a surprise every time. 'I tell them the house was built in 1750, and they meekly say, "Oh really!"'

Anthony Sykes' family home was the eighteenth-century West Park, on the edge of the West Country, on the borders of Hampshire, Dorset and Wiltshire. It had been built in 1720, with wings added by Sir Robert Taylor in 1760, but, like so many country houses, it was pulled down after the Second World War. Anthony is a builder, so it is perhaps no surprise that, in creating a new family seat, he planned and supervised a new property to his own design. He acquired 60 ha (150 acres) of Dorset downland, a completely virgin site. Planning permission had already been granted for a different house (never built), so they were able to go ahead without too much difficulty. Anthony chose this particular spot because it is at the base of a natural amphitheatre, providing some valuable protection from the winds. The property is named Bellamont House, after Bellamont Forest, the first classical building in Ireland.

When it came to the design, there was almost too much choice. Given no space restrictions, a breathtaking setting, and a blank piece of paper, even the most talented of architects might have felt a little taxed. 'Everything came to mind!' says Anthony. In order to have a starting point he returned to the past, and, fittingly, chose to use the footprint of West Park as a template for the new house. With slight modifications, the dimensions of 36 m (120 ft) long by 14 m (46 ft) deep are almost identical to the old family home. Yet this is where the resemblance stops. The exterior of West Park was strictly classical, whereas this building, with its fanciful castellated style, has the echo of the Baroque-inspired Gothick look, which was something of a trademark for the eighteenth century.

Inside, however, he has turned the traditional concept of English country-house living on its head. 'I wanted a home for twenty-first-century living - one that was comfortable, sociable and warm.' In pursuit of that, Anthony returned to the mediaeval concept of the great hall, a vast room, the focus of life, in which people would eat, cook and socialize. He also looked at today's domestic norm, with the kitchen as the hub of the home. The result is one huge room called the Saloon, stretching the full length of the two-storey main block; it is an amazing 14.5 m (56ft) long. It has comfortable sofas, occasional chairs and tables, and a well-concealed galley kitchen at one end. Instead of bringing the sitting room into the kitchen, Anthony and Harriet have done the reverse. They comment that they can watch TV in here, entertain guests, play backgammon, and relax. The secret is a really good and silent extractor fan.

If the concept for the Saloon is modern and refreshing, the planning of its space has been thoroughly traditional. The room is designed according to the strict classical Palladian principles beloved by eighteenth-century architects. Symmetry is the order of the day. Anthony explains that the room is composed of one central cube (with two corners knocked off), measuring over 7m (24 ft) long, wide.

To either side, there are two further cubes, each measuring 5 m (16 ft). And to complete the balanced proportions, there are four tall sash windows and two pairs of double doors leading into the Library from the entrance hall. At the centre of the Library bay is the way through to the Octagon, an inspired modern-day equivalent of an orangery. With its five windows, each one 3 m (10 ft) high, and a domed glass oculus, it is a thoroughly beautiful room, often bathed in sunshine all day long, and looking out across formal terraces to left and right, or due south across the park. It can be used as a separate dining room, or to escape the wind on a bright but blowy day.

It's enlightening to hear Anthony describing the architectural decoration of the Saloon in the context of the rest of the house. He confidently attributes its painted classical columns, ornate cornice and marble fireplace to the style of the prominent Regency architect Sir Jeffry Wyatville (1766-1840). Yet pass through one of the double doors, back into the imposing entrance hall, and the style is from the mid eighteenth century. This, says Anthony, is pure William Kent (1685-1748), an architect particularly well known for his work on the Horse Guards building in London's Whitehall. Yet were an architectural purist to query the fact that the Sykeses have cherry-picked their

OPPOSITE *In bronze lettering above the iron-studded double doors of the main entrance is the family motto;* Coute Que Coute, *which loosely translates as Whatever the Cost.*

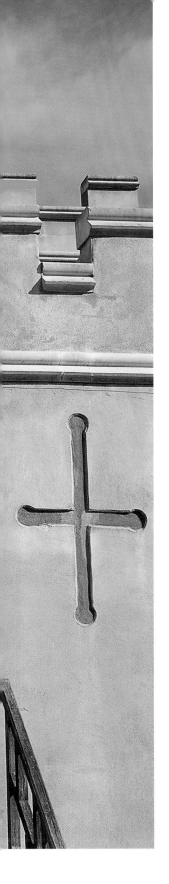

favourite styles, they would be wrong. Every house evolves across time, and becomes the sum of many architectural parts.

The hall, certainly, has the element of surprise that the great English entrance hall has always set out to achieve. The visitor passes through the front doors into a vestibule with classical alcoves, each one accommodating a statue of a Roman hospitality goddess. Then into the hall itself - immensely imposing, with a ceiling 8 m (26 ft) high, a galleried first floor and a stone fireplace over which hangs a circular display of swords. The floor is eighteenth-century style, in Portland stone punctuated with black slate keys.

Because it was a deliberate decision to design a very formal hall, it is fitting, perhaps, that you must pass through an arch to the left or right of the fireplace, in order to arrive in the more relaxed atmosphere of the Saloon. Being a twenty-first-century house, there is no place at Bellamont for draughty corridors.

Instead, much of the floor space that, in a period property, would have been devoted to passages,

LEFT The Octagon, with its floor-to-ceiling central windows, is used for dining. The iron studded doors to either side, lead into parallel formal gardens. The effect of arrow slits was created by attaching wooden templates prior to rendering; when removed, these left realistic depressions. From the stone bench, there's a view down the avenue, to uninterrupted parkland beyond.

butler's pantries, wine stores and the like, has been deliberately devoted to more flexible accommodation. The ground-floor west wing can be a self-contained living area, with two bedrooms, a bathroom, kitchen and sitting room. It can equally double as a guest suite, or a granny flat, or a nursery. In the east wing there is an office, a laundry, another sitting room and a garage. 'So the house provides a flexible template,' says Anthony. Upstairs in the central block there are four principal bedrooms and three bathrooms leading off the balcony on the first floor.

If Bellamont House has been, in part, about paying homage to eighteenth-century architecture, but with a modern-day twist, then the theme is played out in the gardens, too. They are formal, but distinctly minimalist. Stand in the Octagon, and you can look left to the east garden, discreetly paved in local Portland stone. Look to the right, and there are simple lawns. Each formal terrace is bisected symmetrically with a rill, culminating in a stone fountain. There are good reasons for not planting extensive gardens. The Sykeses like to see their cattle and sheep grazing close to the house. As for whether they miss the experience of living in an authentically old building - they don't. Bellamont House, they say, feels perfectly eighteenth century. Even better, it has all the atmosphere of a 250-year-old house, with none of the drawbacks.

ABOVE

The vestibule has been designed with two classical alcoves: in each one, stands a statue of the Roman hospitality goddesses, Flora and Ceres. The walls are wallpapered with faux stone. To the right sits a Charles II travelling trunk, and opposite is a gilded chair, originally designed by Lorenzo Santi for Napoleon's uncle.

OPPOSITE

Linking the vestibule to the hall is pair of semi-glazed double doors. The Sykeses wanted to create a grand hall in the traditional manner. Many portraits line the walls: to the left hangs a portrait of Sir Jocelyn Percy, painted by Cornelius Jansen, and to the right, there is a portrait of the Infanta Maria Anna, daughter of Philip III, By Baretomé Gonzalez.

LEFT & ABOVE

The grand hall is dominated by a display of fifty swords above the stone fireplace. To one side of it is a portrait of the brother of the first Earl of Bellamont, while the portait on the adjacent wall is of Harriet Sykes's great uncle, the eleventh Duke of St Albans and his sisters. Below is a pair of Egyptian figures, in the manner of Thomas Hope. The swans are Davenport ware, and designed to hold eggs; they were a once common sight in dairies up and down the country. Also in the hall is a portrait of Sir Eyre Coote, who was Commander-in-Chief in India. The floor throughout is Portland stone with black slate keys, in the eighteenth-century style of octagon en carre.

ABOVE

In the drawing room, the fireplace is eighteenth-century marble, inlaid with Sicilian jasper. To either side, as in the hall, there are family portraits: on the left, a painting of Anthony's mother and her sister, and on the right, his uncle as a child. A total of twenty marble-effect columns (they are actually wallpapered) were added to emphasize the height and generous proportions of the room. A carved mirror reflects one pair of the double doors that lead into the room, and hangs above a marble-topped console table, which is in the manner of William Kent. Either side of it is a series of family portraits.

RIGHT

Looking from the kitchen area towards the library area, it's possible to see the south-facing windows along the left-hand wall. Marked by the Venetian blackamoor, dated 1800, is the entrance to the Octagon. Clustered on the walls are many family portraits and ornate mirrors. The Gothick bookcase at the far end of the room was bought by Anthony and it has been copied by him a number of times.

OPPOSITE & ABOVE

The sweeping staircase is decorated with impressive swan finials (swans are on the family crest). Since there were only three carved wooden swans – bought from a London shop – Anthony cut the third one in two, and used the divided halves over the half-newels. The staircase walls are lined with twenty pictures of generals who served in the Napoleonic wars, to echo the military theme of the hall. On the turn of the stairs, there is a portrait of Sir Eyre Coote as a younger man, flanked by a pair of plaster classical urns.

LEFT & ABOVE

In summer the full-length sash windows of the Octagon stand open to allow access to the two parallel formal gardens. One is simply paved with Portland stone, with an early Victorian iron bench in the lea of a high yew hedge. From this formal terrace, a door leads on to open parkland.

OVERLEAF

Set into a sheltering coomb of chalk down, the garden front of Bellamont House faces due south, towards the sea. The three windows of the master bedroom, in the central bay, look right out across the park.

INDEX

Page numbers in *italics* refer
to captions/illustrations

ACKNOWLEDGEMENTS

We would like to extend grateful thanks to the owners of the houses featured in this book, for both their patience and their hospitality.

CAROLINE ASHWORTH LAMPSHADES
Blyth Valley Industrial Estate
Halesworth
Suffolk, IP19 8EN
Tel: +44 (0)1986 874 417
Fax: +44 (0)1986 875 519

ELMS LESTERS GALLERY
- TRIBAL ART
1-2-3 Flitcroft Street
London, WC2H 8DH
Tel: +44 (0)20 7836 6747

INDIGO
- DECORATIVE ANTIQUES
FROM THE EAST
275 New Kings Rd
London, SW6 4RD
Tel: +44 (0)20 7384 3101

ARTIQUE
- ANTIQUES
Tallboys House
Church Street
Tetbury, GL8 8JG
Tel: +44 (0)1666 503597

RICHARD HOWARD
Fauconberges Antiques
8 Smallgate
Beccles
Suffolk, NR34 9AD
Tel: +44 (0)1502 716 147

DAVID MENDEL
- SPECIALIST PAINTER
AND COLOUR CONSULTANT
Westbrook House
West Bradley
Somerset, BA6 8LF
Tel: +44 (0)1458 850604

KEITH ANDERSON
- GARDEN DESIGNER
Westbrook House
West Bradley
Somerset BA6 8LF
Tel: +44 (0)1458 850604

JEFFREY PICK
- DECORATIVE PAINTER
Clarence Villa
5 Spinners Walk
Windsor
Berkshire, SL4 3AR.
Tel/Fax: +44 (0)1753 853628
Mobile: +44 (0)7985 330424

PENWOOD NURSERIES LTD
- MR DOUGLAS HARRIS
The Drove
Penwood
Newbury
Berkshire, RG20 89EW
Tel: +44 (0)1635 254366

RORY YOUNG
- LIME & PLASTER REPAIRS AND
STONE CONSERVATION
7 Park Street
Cirencester
Gloucestershire, GL7 2BX

JUDITH VERITY
- STONE MASONS
Jubilee Chapel
Startley
Chippenham
Wiltshire, SN15 5RG

BARRY SULLIVAN
- GENERAL BUILDING AND
CONSERVATION WORK
47 Kingscourt Lane
Strous
Gloucestershire, GL5 3QR

DAVID MLINARIC
- INTERIOR DESIGN CONSULTANT
38 Bourne Street
London, SW1W 8JA

OWLPEN MANOR,
Dursley,
Gloucestershire, GL11 5BZ
Telephone: +44 (0)1453 860261
Fax: +44 (0)1453 860819
email: sales@owlpen.com
website: www.owlpen.com
*Owlpen Manor is open from 1st April to
30 September Tuesday to Sunday 2pm to 5pm.
Restaurant opens at 12 noon.*

ANTHONY JAGGARD
- ARCHITECT
John Stark & Ptns
13 Princes Street
Dorchester
Tel: +44 (0)1305 262636

BELLAMONT TOPIARY BOXTREE
NURSERY
Tel/Fax +44 (0)1308 482220
Email: harriet@bellamont-topiary.co.uk

GUINEVERE ANTIQUES
578 Kings Road
London, SW6
Tel: +44 (0)20 7736 2917

PETA SMYTHE
- ANTIQUE TEXTILES
42 Morton Street
London, SW1
Tel: +44 (0)20 7603 9898

HOLKHAM NURSERY GARDENS
Holkham Park
Wells next the Sea
Norfolk, NR23 1AB
tel: +44 (0)1328 711 636
http://www.holkhamgardens.com

VEERE GRENNEY
- INTERIOR DESIGNER
1b Hollywood Road
London, SW10 9HS
Tel: +44 (0)20 7351 7170
veere@veeregrenney.co.uk

THE ROMANTIC GARDEN NURSERY
Swannington
Norwich, NR9 5NW
Tel: +44 (0)1603 261488

GLEBE FARM HEDGING
Glebe
Langham
Colchester, CO4 5PP
Tel: +44 (0)1206 323200

THE CHELSEA GARDENER
123 Sydney Street
London, SW3 6NR
Tel: +44 (0)20 7351 2388

PHOEBE HART
- SPECIALIST RUG MAKER
The Studio
East Street
Lewes
Sussex
Tel: +44 (0)1273 478791

MYRIAD ANTIQUES
13 Portland Road
London, W11
Tel: +44 (0)20 7229 1709

GEORGE CARTER
- GARDEN DESIGNER
gcarter@easynet.co.uk